BOTTOM SIDE UP

Breaking Open,
Falling Apart,
Comimg Back as Something Else....

LINDA S. WHITE

Copyright © 2013 Linda S. White

All rights reserved.

ISBN: 1489546146

ISBN 13: 9781489546142

Library of Congress Control Number: 2013909821
CreateSpace Independent Publishing Platform
North Charleston, South Carolina

a Story of
Breaking Open
Falling Apart
Coming Back as Something Else

The memoirs of a Chamber of Commerce chief, struggling to find the meaning of life during the dozen years between the attacks of September 11 and the post-Great Recession meltdown

In 2009, at the epicenter of the economic meltdown, a local Chamber of Commerce Chief is forced to close the Chamber of Commerce, an organization she built through the mergers of three chambers and where she served for over a decade. Her husband loses his job on the same day, and sixty days later, they are faced with taking custody of their eight-year-old special-needs grandson.

Caught in the confusing crosscurrents of career, friendships, economics, family, politics, and religion, she tries to find meaning in a world that has turned *Bottom Side Up*.

Drawing on the strength of her farming roots, a nurturing relationship with her mother, and a sense of community belonging, she seeks to find balance, meaning and a second wind as she journeys through the "narrows" from prominence to anonymity.

To Mama
When I'm lost, your love and wisdom help me remember who I am.

ACKNOWLEDGMENTS

Bottom Side Up was written and shared in honor of all of us who are or have ever been *Bottom Side Up*. (And that's most of us.)

I am grateful to all who have trusted me with their personal *Bottom Side Up* stories. Our stories are our medicine. Your stories made me feel less alone and gave me courage to move through the tangled parts of my own life—if for no other reason than to reach back, catch your hand, and pull you toward my light.

To my wonderful friends from the Transformation Tribe who gave me the courage to write and publish this book.

To Helen, Sandy, and Georgette, former chamber of commerce employees and three of the strongest, most beautiful women I know. They taught me everything that is right about women and leadership in the workplace. They only ever asked me for two things: to tell them the truth and to allow them to discover and live their own truth.

And I did.

They rode out on their own horse—whole, strong, loving, and beautiful.

And they still are.

*Our Stories
Are Our Medicine*

—CLARISSA PINKOLA ESTES, *WOMEN WHO RUN WITH WOLVES*

CONTENTS

Acknowledgments vii
Foreward xiii
The *Bottom Side Up* Handbook xvii
About Me xix
Introduction xxv
Part One: Breaking Open 1
    2001 3
    2002 13
    Life before the Crack 17
    2003 21
    2004 29
    2005 36
    2006 50
    2007 59
    2008 69
    2009 75
Part Two: Falling Apart 97
    2010 128
    2011 136
Part Three: Coming Back as Something Else 155
    2012 157
    2013 184
    Epilogue 195

FOREWARD

"We are the ones we've been waiting for."

—HOPI ELDER PRAYER

As I finish the last pages of this book, the TV news is covering yet another tragic event in America—the devastating and historic Oklahoma tornado. It happened yesterday, but the father of a still-missing third-grader quietly sits on a stool, awaiting news.

The media reports that there were "tears quietly cascading down his face as he awaited any news."

Another stunned survivor questions, "How did this happen? Why did this happen? How do we explain this to the kids?... In an instant, everything is gone...."

And indeed, it is.

These kinds of tragedies have broken us open so many times recently. We engage unsuccessfully in making sense of the Aurora, Colorado shootings, the Sandy Hook massacre, the Boston Marathon bombings, and other more personal and not-so-public tragedies: the loss of a job, the betrayal of a spouse, the indifference of public officials, the drug addiction of a family member, the abuse by parents who even kill their own children, the slaying of a police officer, gunned down in the line of duty, or the diagnosis of a life-threatening illness.

We try to understand.

We don't.

We can't.

But we must go on.

As human beings trying desperately to survive, we must run toward our pain—not away from it. As communities, we must begin the intentional act of administering the medicine of courage and compassion and hope to our broken souls and polarized communities.

There is no other way. After all, we are all in this together.

The world is far too chaotic for us to bear without each other: without the engagement and support of compassionate and highly trained emergency responders, mental health practitioners, clergy, neighbors, families, and communities. We must learn to engage together and then circle back again and again to each other until we have poured compassion, courage, and resilience into every individual, family, and community in America.

We must reclaim our ability to act with courage and compassion even when—and especially when—sadness and confusion rise in front of us in epic scenes, bearing the face of unspeakable sorrow. Jaded by the breakdown within our current systems, I am left cynical about our current state of affairs—but not about our future. Fortunately, I still have incredible faith in the American people and their resilience.

We have seen unselfish acts of courage and compassion played out over and over in tragedies that have plagued us over the past few years. Even as we speak to the failures of the education system, we witness teachers who use their own bodies to cover and protect children from gunfire and tornadoes.

We have talked of an America that is numbed by Facebook and social media, but in contrast, with tear-filled eyes, we have watched strangers run toward the blasts in the Boston Marathon bombings to care for injured strangers.

Rising from the ashes of each tragedy are a multitude of heroes or angels (you decide): police officers who run directly into harm's way to protect and serve; first responders in Texas who give their lives to save a neighborhood; and a daughter who gives her father a kidney.

Linda S. White

I personally know elected officials who have the courage and the wisdom within their souls to make our communities and our country a better place. They have shared with me their frustration and sadness at the inability to create the kind of community where its people flourish. They must find the courage to break free of systems that no longer serve us *and keep us stuck in a place I've named Bottom Side Up.*

They must choose the right things over the politically correct things.

They must engage in asking the hard questions and finding the new answers.

Education systems must once again start educating American children to compete in a global economy, learning to lean in to those children who are emerging from a *Bottom-Side-Up* economy. The foundation of these children is fragile and fragmented. They are the product of a generation of lost jobs, homeless and displaced families, broken communities, and high rates of parents with mental health and substance-abuse issues. We cannot lose these children too, for they are the future of America.

We must demand a transformation of our health-care systems, creating systems of compassion and creativity, of health and healing. That means that "we the people" must accept personal responsibility for our own health and wellness—as difficult as that is in a fast, supersized world.

We must create new systems where government and law enforcement engage with their people in ways that restore trust and create safe and vibrant communities. Good people should never be afraid of their government or their law enforcement. Bad people should never be allowed to destroy our sense of safety.

Men and women alike must learn new ways of engaging as a family in this brave new world, where the boundaries of gender have been—and will remain—blurred. As families, we must get back to the job of raising our children to be responsible, resilient, productive, and loving.

If we have the courage to break open and fall apart, we can come back as something else—stronger, wiser, and more resilient.

THE *BOTTOM SIDE UP* HANDBOOK

This book is for anyone—and that's most of us—who has ever felt like his or her life somehow got *Bottom Side Up*.

HOW TO USE THIS BOOK

Get it messy.

Write in the margins.

Dog-ear the page corners.

Spill coffee, wine, or your beverage of choice on it. But dammit, read it!

No, I mean really read it.

Share it.

Quote from it.

Underline with highlighters and colored pencils—anything that makes you think, "God, I know that feeling."

Laugh. Cry. Pray. Swear.

Question.

And beyond anything, know that you are okay, *Bottom Side Up* and all!

Bottom Side Up

Have faith that we (that's you and I) and our families and our communities and America can get up again. Dizzy—maybe from being *Bottom Side Up* for so long, our wings still wet from being hunkered down in the dark cocoon, anxious and awkward, wondering if we can ever fly again—but, nonetheless, up and alive with a new way of seeing, a new way of being, and a newfound courage to rebuild our lives.

At the back of this book is a place for your notes. Write in it. Own it. Restory your life here.

So I give you this safe place to sit down with the beverage of your choice—this is, after all, a very grown-up book. Write in the margin of the pages as though you are writing in the edges of your own life. Journey with me through this place of joy and sorrow, anger and forgiveness, shadows and light, despair and hope.

And if you are feeling lonely or confused, reach through the book and take my hand.

I've been where you are:

—breaking open

—falling apart

—coming back as something else

—living in a place called *Bottom Side Up*.

ABOUT ME

I was born and raised in a rural, west Tennessee farming community. The story goes that my mother (Mama) was singing "Amazing Grace" as I was born. My farm life was richly steeped in Southern Baptist tent revivals, gospel singings, church socials, covered dishes, a loving family, southern hospitality, gratitude, and hard work.

My father worked as a civilian security guard for an army ammunition plant by night, and by day, he was a cotton farmer. He lost his job in a massive layoff when I was a young girl, and I mostly knew him as a cotton farmer, which made me a farmer's daughter.

A working farm is like art. With a little luck and a lot of faith, everything is created by you—your food, your shelter, and your livelihood. If you don't create it, you don't have it.

I was an only child and loved being a "tomboy." My mother teased me about being the only boy my father ever had. But she still made me wear lace panties under my overalls and sleep in hair curlers every Saturday night. Sunday mornings, I always wore a frilly dress and curly hair to the Baptist church. Every Saturday, I went to the country store with Daddy, where the men talked about farming and politics. I sang and tapped danced for them, and they bought me RC colas, peanuts, and, sometimes, M&Ms.

One day, I met Martin Luther King as he stopped at the store to get gas on his way to Memphis. Daddy introduced me to him, and Mr. King shook my hand. I still remember that his hand was big and rough to the touch. He told me to "study hard and love everybody." The community farm men told Daddy it wasn't proper to take me out to meet Martin Luther King. Daddy said that he didn't give a hoot what they thought. "That man is goin' to be important to the history of this country. She will remember this day. He's shaping the world she will live in." he told them. And as they say on the farm, "That was that."

Daddy wasn't very educated, but he was really smart. He also prayed a lot, but he didn't go to church much. Daddy was plainspoken and said there were a lot of hypocrites in the church. He said he could talk to God just fine by himself. Despite the fact that he didn't attend church regularly, everybody said that my daddy was a "fine man."

Mama was different. She worried a lot about her wretched soul and welcomed an extra prayer by the preacher on her behalf. She also worried a lot about my wretched soul, which was probably the reason I was baptized in a pond at the age of twelve to the backdrop of the Baptist congregation singing "Shall We Gather at the River." We said grace before meals and prayers before bed. We didn't ask for much. We mostly said, "Thanks."

Mama volunteered a lot in our farming community. She volunteered with the health department during the polio immunization initiative when they put the vaccine on sugar cubes. The county health department held the events on Sunday afternoon at the community school. They even let me set out the little paper cups that held the sugar cubes filled with polio vaccine drops. I was happy that we weren't going to see people in wheelchairs—ever again. This may have been the reason I chose a career in health care, serving in the poorest communities in rural Tennessee. Mama said we should be "real grateful" that our community was going to get the medicine.

I never saw a drop of alcohol in our house. I mostly believed that everyone who drank alcohol was going to hell. That also applied to dancing and card playing and being lazy; although, Daddy proudly claimed that he had once been a "helluva" dancer. Lazy people went to hell the same as drunks (so they said)—maybe to a hotter place. Lazy was very, very bad.

I was twenty-eight the first time I tasted alcohol. It was wine, and I had an allergic reaction. The ER doctor in the hospital where I worked laughed at me and said I would probably grow out of it.

By the way, I did.

My father (Daddy) gave me courage. My mother (Mama) gave me grace.

I was taught to work hard, study hard, pray hard, visit the sick, and do my best—always. Mama read to me from the *Book of Fairy Tales* almost every day. I'm sure Mama never knew how much her love and those stories would shape my life. I was raised chasing fireflies, listening to gospel and country music, eating homemade ice cream, and believing in "happily ever after."

Money played only a small part in the "happily ever afters" that I knew.

I was smart and curious for a farm girl. Mama always said I was too smart for my own good. All of the women I knew were strong and slightly stubborn.

My paternal grandmother had been a "medicine woman" and a midwife. She would go by wagon to tend the sick and deliver babies in the community. Daddy always said I had the same gift of healing that my grandmother had.

I loved reading books about strong women and far-away places. In the summer, the postmistress, Ms. Mozelle McLemore, chose books for me from the regional bookmobile.

The mailman left them one at a time in the mailbox, along with a note from Ms. Mozelle, asking me to write a book report on a five-by-seven note card, which she graciously included in the front of each book. When I returned the book and the report, she sent another book.

My summers were filled with doing farm work, listening to porch stories, and reading books from the bookmobile. Ms. Mozelle always sent books about strong women: Louisa May Alcott, Eleanor Roosevelt, Florence Nightingale, Amelia Earhart, Helen Keller, and Scarlett O'Hara in *Gone with the Wind*. Looking back, I think Mama believed in love, and Ms. Mozelle believed in women being self-sufficient. I grew up believing I could have it all.

Much to my parents' disapproval, my high-school sweetheart and I married young, in the height of the Vietnam war and just before the draft ended. A lot of us got married early during the war. We had a son early into a very short marriage. After the divorce, I went back home to finish growing up. Mama said I had an "early frost."

My son was the light of my life, and my parents absolutely adored him. I worked in a factory and went to school at night. I studied psychology in my early college days, but somehow I couldn't see myself sitting behind a desk, listening to folks talk about their troubles. A farm girl is raised to actually do stuff—not talk about it. Work seemed to me to solve a lot of life's problems. Daddy always said it didn't matter if the water was hot or cold if you had to go through it.

I was lucky enough to find love again. I studied business management, premed and physical rehabilitation at Shelby State and UT Memphis. I chose the hardest internships, working at St. Jude's Children's Hospital and the Elvis Presley Trauma Center in Memphis.

My chosen career took me into rural home health care and public policy, where I lobbied Congress on behalf of medical associations and health-care organizations. My young days of visiting polio patients ("shut-ins") in the community had a profound effect on my adult life. I visited sick families in rural homes without running water. I walked the legislative halls of Nashville, Tennessee and the congressional halls of Washington, DC, lobbying for best-practices legislation and access to health care. Still stubborn and strong-willed, I managed a home health-care agency and took my nurses into the poorest and toughest places, utilizing cutting-edge health care.

I lived a storybook life with a loving husband on a twenty-five-acre bucolic farm. My life was filled with love and laughter and always a Sunday afternoon yard full of friends and great food. I had a successful career, a great family, and a boatload of friends. My husband and I were dreamers and doers. Our friends said we lit up the room when we walked in together—especially when we took to the dance floor two-stepping and waltzing to our favorite song, "We Had It All." And indeed we did.

In 1990, we were taking sailing lessons and planning to buy a sailboat to sail halfway around the world during the millennium year of 2000. We planned to be drinking champagne somewhere on the ocean on New Year's Eve 2000. Our dreams were grand, and I trusted him completely.

But in July of 1990, tragedy struck our lives as our beloved teenage son committed suicide.

The grief was devastating and within six months of our son's death, our storybook marriage ended, taking with it my "happily ever after." My grieving father died a few months later. Within the span of a few months, I had lost the three men in my life that I most adored.

My mother and I were devastated. Broken and grieving, we were all that was left of our "happily ever after." I was too devastated to even cry. Mama said that she never understood that. She cried for years. I kept the farm and worked harder than ever in health care, public policy, and government relations. Caring for others was my medicine. Mama took pills and prayed. I worked three jobs. I was a farm girl. It was all I knew to do. I was afraid I would run out of pills before I ran out of pain. Somehow, I was propelled through the horrendous grief by my work, the love of my friends and family, the "happily ever after" stories from my mother, and the books about strong women that the postmistress sent me. I found no comfort from the bible.

I was mad at God anyway. But I did believe that if a heart could be broken, it must also possess the capacity to heal; although, at the time, I could not imagine how. So I worked day and night and hoped the pain would one day go away.

The pain of trying to live in the same place where I had loved—without the people that I had loved—was at times almost unbearable. Their memories haunted me from every direction. In late 1993, I sold my beloved farm and most of my belongings and moved to Florida, where I married my husband Jerry, the nicest man in the world. It was the place where I would try to start over.

I promised my mother that I would always be there for her—no matter how far away I was or whatever happened.

I left Tennessee with Mama sitting on the doorstep crying. But we both needed a change. Florida seemed so far away from Mama, Friday-night football, childhood friends, and my southern roots. It also seemed so far away from the place where I had loved and lost. Perhaps in Florida, near the ocean, in the land of sunshine, I could forget.

And it is here that I begin my story.

INTRODUCTION
Why I Wrote This Book

I have a duty to speak the truth as I see it
And share not just my triumphs,
Not just the things that felt good,
But the pain—
The intense unmitigated pain.
It is important to share how I know
That survival is survival
And not just a walk in the rain.

—AUDRE LORDE

Okay, so here I am.

It's 2013, and I thought that by now I would be living on Easy Street, traveling to romantic, adventurous places and perhaps writing a book—but definitely not this book. Instead, I find myself, career in flux, living in Florida, in an edge city also called a commuter community located between the shadow of Orlando's "Big Mouse" and the sand and sun of the Atlantic Ocean.

It sounds likes a great place, right?

The problem is that it is one of the many "Ground Zeros of the Great Economic Meltdown." It is in the Sun Belt, the place where most of us are *Bottom Side Up*. And so I find myself forced to re-story my life, because the one I planned many years ago isn't working anymore. When it first happened, I cursed and cried and protested "why me?" and "what did I ever do to deserve this?"

But sitting in the workshop for newly unemployed people, the guy next to me said, "What did you used to be?" I said that I ran a chamber of commerce, and he said, "Wow, are you shitting me? I guess it's happening to everybody." He said that he used to be a chef before he lost his job. And that explained why he kept using hand sanitizer between filling out forms. I thought at first that he was obsessive compulsive—nope. Just like most of us in the unemployment workshop, we were all just *Bottom Side Up*.

One lady suggested that I get my doctor to prescribe some pain pills. "It makes it a lot easier."

Without emotion, she shared, "It keeps you kinda chilled out, because the rejection you get when you send out resumes is terrible."

Shaking my head no, I replied, "Yeah, that doesn't so much work for me," because "not working" and "not feeling" was just like being dead to me. So I rolled out of my "fetal-question-mark-ball of why" and decided to start writing about what it's like to be *Bottom Side Up*.

And one day I decided to share it with you. Perhaps I can give a voice and a name to our confusion and pain. Maybe I can give all of us a place to lay out our messies, because we can't get through it until we process it. And I really don't like zombies! So, own your messies. Name them. Count them. Talk about them. Curse them. Pray about them. Grieve them.

Cry about them. Laugh about them.

And then perhaps one day, we will all be able to put them behind us and start over. Just maybe we can all find the courage to get right-side-up again.

So sit here with me and write in the margins of your own life as I take you through my journey of *breaking open-falling apart-and finally coming back as something else.*

Linda S. White

I hope you will be inspired to once again believe in yourself, your family, and your community as I share with you my personal story of how I came to be in a very dark place that I named *Bottom Side Up*. And how—after many, many moons—I finally turned toward the light and emerged as something else: restoried, smiling, radically grateful, fiercely independent, wiser, more loving, simple, and spilling over with compassion and creativity. It is my sincerest hope that you too will find the courage to reclaim and re-story your own life on your own terms.

*Why do you go away?
So that you can come back.
So that you can see the place you came from
with new eyes and extra colors.*

*And the people there see you differently too.
Coming back to where you started is not the
same as never leaving.*

—TERRY PRATCHETT, "A HAT FULL OF SKY"

PART ONE

Breaking Open

"Life is like an egg. Once it's broken open, it's never the same again."

—LINDA WHITE

2001

It was a beautiful, ordinary, sunny day in September. It seems that most bad days start out beautiful and ordinary—at least most of mine have.

My husband, Jerry, was working for a global manufacturing technology company, where he had worked for twenty-five years as a computer network manager. I was chief executive officer at a regional chamber of commerce in central Florida, a place nestled between the "Big Mouse" in Orlando and the Atlantic Ocean in Daytona Beach, right in the heart of the sun belt—the place where the economy seemed to be booming. The construction and real estate market was driving the economy.

The governments (which I will refer to later in this book as "HAL") were fat and happy. I was in an area that had incorporated two new cities in less than a decade. Part of my job as a chamber chief was to argue against the creation of so many business regulations, so I was happy too. We didn't talk about it much, but we were already losing high-tech and manufacturing jobs. Tourism, government, construction, and the housing and commercial real estate market were fast becoming the main engines of economic growth in our county. Indeed, it was producing a good tax base for HAL (the government). That scenario would later become the source of our economic meltdown.

It was Tuesday, and I dressed that morning in a navy-blue suit. I was chairing a tourism meeting that began at 7:30 a.m. I arrived on time, smiling as usual (that's my nature), and ready to rumble.

I was a bit of a thorn in the side of the tourism authority. The chamber was running a visitors' information center, and I wanted some of the bed-tax funds to run my visitors' center—the only one in our area. Every other chamber of commerce in the county got bed-tax funds—except for ours. Two of the three newly incorporated cities in my region were edge cities and commuter communities. They hardly ever got the kinds of things that the more established, traditional cities got. Incorporation had not made that better. If our cities were to progress as vibrant communities, I would have to change the philosophy, which would necessitate that I would live like a salmon swimming upstream and tilting at windmills. The more established "powers that be" weren't too keen on sharing with the new guys in town. I was a main player on the "newcomers'" team. That made me disadvantaged from the beginning. But more about that later....

Around eight thirty that morning, my cell phone started vibrating—a lot. In fact, it seemed that everybody's phones were vibrating. We weren't texting then, and I didn't have a smartphone, so I wasn't getting e-mails. The meeting adjourned around eight forty-five, and everybody hurried out the door to answer their calls. I listened to the voice mails as I drove the ten-minute drive back to my office.

Jerry had left a message that a plane had crashed into the World Trade Center, and that it looked bad. I didn't think much about the message. I was wondering if I was going to be able to get bed-tax money for my visitors' center and thinking about the busy day ahead. I had a chamber board of directors' meeting scheduled for five thirty that evening. Board-meeting days were always hectic. I had the greatest board of directors in the world. I loved them like my best friends and lovingly referred to them as the "suits."

Linda S. White

We had a Washington, DC fly-in scheduled for the early part of October, and I made a mental note to check if everyone that was going had finished their security screening. I needed to bring that up at the board meeting.

I walked in the door to my office right at 9:00 a.m. My entire staff was standing in the middle of the conference room floor, glued to the TV. Sandy, my office manager, started telling me that a plane had crashed into the World Trade Center. Still not paying attention or understanding what was happening, I began talking to one of my chamber members who had just dropped in to pay her dues.

I always liked when the chamber members stopped by to chat. She was in our leadership class, and I had noticed one of the guys in the class making some "off-color" remarks to her.

Our policy was to let the leadership class handle their own issues. That's part of leadership—learning to handle uncomfortable situations—and that was one of the many ways we stretched them to make them stronger. But I wanted to address the issue with her just the same. (Women leaders support other women when they can, and I wanted her to know that.) I asked her if he was making her uncomfortable, and that if he was, she should speak up. She was laughing and telling me that she could handle the situation. It was then that we heard Sandy scream, "Oh my God, there's another one."

We quickly ran to where they were standing. Sandy—in her Boston accent that tends to get very fast when she's excited—tried to help me understand what was happening. From the beginning, she realized that this was no accident.

"Sandy, are you telling me that they're deliberately crashing planes into the World Trade Center and the Pentagon?" We could only stare into the TV with disbelief and utter, "Oh my God."

The rest of that day is America's history, but it was also the day that changed everything—forever. That night, we cancelled our board meeting and did what most of America did: we went home to hold our families and try to make sense of the senseless events of the day.

As the hours and days unfolded before us, we felt increasingly violated and vulnerable. Our America and its people were wounded, scared, and sad. Feeling a deep sense of uneasiness, we wondered what was next. I guess that's why we call it terror.

Back at the Chamber, we had a ribbon cutting and grand opening scheduled for Thursday morning for a new business. Though most of us were still in shock, I made the decision to conduct business as usual. I am a farm girl, and I believe that showing up to work solves a lot of the world's problems. Daddy always said, "It doesn't matter if the water is hot or cold if you have to go through it." We couldn't just stay hunkered down forever.

And so with all the inspiration and courage I could muster, I called our chamber ambassador team together and begged them to come out and do the ribbon cutting. I did not always attend the ribbon cuttings. Our chamber ambassador team usually handled that duty, but obviously, that morning, I went. It was one of those times when I watched "from without and within."

I could feel it all—my own anxiety, the sadness of America, the fear in our community, and the uncertainty of this new businessman who had risked it all for the American dream of owning his own business. I felt anxious and vulnerable. Fifteen people showed up that morning to welcome and support the new business. I could only imagine what was going through this local businessman's mind. He had mortgaged his home for a small business loan and had started a business, only to find himself in the middle of a terrorist attack on America a week after he had opened. His American dream had quickly become an American nightmare. He told me how grateful he was that we had been there for him, and that I had let him talk about his fears not only for America but for himself.

He spoke so honestly: "Linda, I know it's selfish to think about myself with everything around us like it is, but I do. I worry if I'm going to be able to make this business work. What's going to happen to us? And thank you for coming out this morning and supporting me. It means a lot."

I smiled reassuringly. "Anything you need—let me know. We're here for you." I was truly glad that we were able to support him, even in a small way. It fed the "craving for meaning" that I so often searched for in my life. It was the lingering question after the death of my son: "Why am I here?"

By now, the ambassador team was eating pastries, drinking coffee, and doing what they do so well—merrymaking. I was grateful for them and proud. I hugged them all and told them so. The world needed a whole big ambassador team!

The weekend didn't make things better. I called Mama in Tennessee twice a day, which wasn't all that unusual anyway. She was the one I always wanted when things went *Bottom Side Up*—I don't care if I am grown. She's also the one who gave me the southern drawl that I try not to use so much if I'm talking about important stuff. And that's also when it usually slips out—it's one of my shortcomings. (Word of caution: don't be fooled by it.)

As the days passed after 9-11, we found that we had more questions than answers. We sat glued to the TV news. Finally, on Saturday night, I said to Jerry, "I've got to get out of the house—away from this TV. I was feeling nauseous and lightheaded. I was pretty sure it was anxiety. Somehow I felt like I was supporting the victims by watching the devastation, but I was becoming afraid and anxious, which wasn't doing anybody any good.

America was beginning to feel small and powerless. That was not a good thing. We couldn't let that happen. We went out to eat, but the restaurant, which had a TV on, was packed with people, probably just like me, trying to run from anxiety. Almost everyone was drinking an alcoholic beverage and looking very somber—most tried not to look up at the TV. Getting out of the house helped a little, but I was glad to get back to the safety of home. I stayed there the rest of the weekend and tried not to watch so much TV.

Back at the chamber office on Monday, it seemed as though we were still moving in slow motion. I had made the decision to cancel our

Washington fly-in, which was scheduled for the early part of October. I doubted we would be allowed into the capitol or to visit with any of the congressmen anyway. We coordinated the fly-in with our district congressman, who served as the very powerful republican leader of the House Transportation and Infrastructure Committee.

After the September 11 attacks, he led the effort to restore stability to the aviation industry and co-authored the aviation and transportation bill. I was sure he was going to be overwhelmed for some time to come, just trying to restore air travel in this brave new world.

I contacted the board Chairman and Vice Chairman and, without hesitation, they both agreed that we should cancel the trip. We might not be able to get our refunds, but we didn't care. We weren't about to fly anywhere anytime soon—much less to Washington, DC.

That Monday, national leaders were still trying to get Wall Street back open and the air transportation system functioning again. I could only imagine the chaos. Around nine o'clock, I contacted the travel agency about canceling our flight. The agent said that she wasn't sure if we could get our money back. They were just trying to deal with the travel plans of the day as the airlines resumed service. She said that she would let me know when she had more information.

Sandy, my sassy office manager from Boston, was chattering about "the evil bastads" and how she hoped somebody found them and made them pay. "Bastads" is Boston drawl for *bastards*.

Sandy always leaves off the *R*s—especially when she's mad.

Heidi, who also worked at the Chamber, was the "kind heart" of our bunch. Mother of four—including a set of twins—loving, and always soft spoken, she teared up when speaking about the victims and their families. I loved how Heidi loved everybody. And everybody who came into the chamber loved her. She was just the kind of person I wanted the visitors to see.

Sandy and Heidi had been with me as long as I had been with the Chamber, except for a brief time when Sandy's husband died, and she took another job to get health insurance. I later managed to get a health-care policy for us and begged her to come back. I loved telling them every day at closing time, "See you tomorrow." The September 11 event was a reminder of how fragile life really is. Sometimes there is no tomorrow.

Sandy and Heidi were comfortable enough with me to express whatever was on their minds. The other three staff members, whom I had acquired in a recent merger, were quieter about the whole thing. I let each of them work at their own pace.

We gathered around the conference table for our usual Monday morning team meeting. I encouraged my marketing director to ease off the fundraising for a bit. We had our annual Autumn Festival coming up in October, so the fundraising was in full swing. She lamented that we would fall short on budget, and since she got commission on all her sponsorship sales, it would hit her paycheck.

I was already worried that the economy would be deeply affected. The interesting thing about a chamber of commerce is that it feels everything the community feels. That's why chambers are such good dashboards of current reality and why a chamber chief is called upon so much for "sense making." This was going to cause a lot of paychecks to be cut. I could already feel it.

Fear is a terrible thing for the economy.

Aggravated, but not at her, I not-so-tactfully answered, "This is a tragic epic event. People are on edge. I'm on edge. We need to just give it a rest." I knew we needed the event money to make our payroll, but I just couldn't see talking to our chamber members about sponsoring a festival—at least not right now. The group became quiet. They were searching my face for some clue as how to proceed. I was struggling with that myself. I scanned all the events for the week, grappling with the appropriate response to a world that had completely turned *Bottom Side Up*.

I made a note to call my best friend and longtime county commissioner (for purposes of this book, I'll call her "Sage," not her real name) to discuss what to do about our leadership class. Sage was not only a great supporter of the chamber but my best friend. She was smart and strong and politically powerful. I was glad she had chosen to help me get things done in the community. It made struggling to build community into these newly incorporated commuter cities easier. They were in her district, so it also helped her politically, which made her happy. She lived and breathed politics. That's why she was so good at it. Sage and I had developed a leadership program and were in the middle of a very successful launch with twenty leadership students. Suddenly, the curriculum we had set up seemed to pale in light of the events. I needed to process with her—later.

We closed the team meeting that day, still a little uncertain as how to handle the events of the week. I told the staff it would be a difficult week. We would take it a day at a time. I planned a phone bank that week to call as many of our members as possible—just to reassure them. It was my way of taking the pulse of the community. I poured a strong cup of coffee and headed back to my office to make a few more calls and ponder how to go forward. I was still reeling and scared, although I wouldn't admit it. When you're the leader, you can never let 'em see you sweat.

It was right around ten forty-five when Heidi came to my door and said, "Linda, the Congressman is on line two for you."

"You mean *his office*?" I asked—a bit startled.

"No, I mean the Congressman."

He was the congressman for our district and one of the more powerful congressional leaders in DC. I was sure she was mistaken. How could a congressman, particularly such a powerful one with such important responsibilities today, possibly be on the phone, asking for me in the middle of all this chaos? So I picked up the phone, and the voice on the other end was indeed the congressman himself, direct and to the point.

"Good morning, sir. How can I help you? I'm sure you must be really busy today."

"Yes, Linda, I am busy today," he replied. "I understand you cancelled your fly-in."

I thought to myself, *Oh my God, how did he know, and why did he care?*

"Listen to me. I need you to get your people together and get on that plane and fly to Washington. Do you understand? How do you think we can resume air travel if people are afraid to fly? I don't have to explain to you the impact to the economy if we don't start moving again. You are a community leader, and it's people like you all over America that need to show courage right now. If you show fear, the terrorists win. And listen to me, we are not bowing down to them." He was fierce!

By now the tears were streaming down my face.

He pressed, "Can you get your people together and get on a plane and fly up here, or do you need me to call them?"

"No, sir, I can make it happen."

"Now you go out and show some leadership in the community," he urged.

The lump in my throat left me almost speechless. Before he hung up, and with tears running down my face, I managed to mutter, "Thank you."

"You're welcome."

"Be safe, sir; we'll see you soon."

And we did see him soon. Fifteen of us boarded a plane on an early October morning before daylight and headed to Washington DC. We would be one of the first community groups to reenter the capitol after September 11. I had been there many times before, but today was really the first time I saw and understood America in all its freedom and splendor.

Though I had been to DC many times, the visibly large army of security presence was new to me. Looking down the barrel of their military-style weapons, I realized that we had lost a bit of what we in America cherish so much—our freedom. The Capitol Police seemed fierce and were obviously on high alert. It was obvious that they were very uncomfortable with a group of us being in their midst. I could sense that they would much rather we go away. They seemed slightly aggravated that the congressman had brought us in, and they cautioned us to stay close together. They gave us strict orders that no one should wander off away from the group. Our presence was no doubt a distraction in what was still a very tense situation.

Our Congressman pushed us to engage—bold, fearless, and proud. And I understood what he knew all along: that freedom really is fragile. When fear kicks in, freedom can be lost in an instant. And I also came to understand that the balance between safety and freedom is a very thin line. I loved America more that day than any other day in my life. I was proud of my board ("the suits") and my congressman. How lucky I was to be able to serve our community alongside such brave and noble people and to be governed by a congressman that was so committed to freedom and connected to the people he served.

Though we tried hard not to let September 11 change us, it did. And that was the event that really started our journey into the place I named *Bottom Side Up*.

2002
The Crack Begins

Our egg—and that included our "nest egg"—actually began to crack in 2002 when my husband Jerry was working for a global high tech manufacturing company in Florida. He had worked there for twenty-six faithful years as a computer network manager. He loved his job, his coworkers, and the Corporation.

His life plan was to work for the Corporation as long as he could, retire, get the gold watch, and fish happily ever after on the St. Johns River (the river that runs north). The quiet waves of change, both global and personal, began to wash over us as the engineers began getting RIF (reduction-in-force) notices. Whoever thought that high-tech engineers in America would get laid off? Let me rephrase that: whoever thought that technical engineers working in America for a worldwide high-tech manufacturing company would get RIF notices?

The odd thing was that they (the engineers) were being forced to train their foreign-worker replacements. These foreign workers were taking the high-paying engineer jobs for far less money. Everybody knew that stuff was "un-American" and just plain bullshit, and they said so—loudly and proudly. The American engineers started flying little American flags on top of their cubicles. They protested to chambers of commerce, elected officials, and media outlets. Much to my surprise, the outrage never got traction. Some said it was just the aligning and adjustment of the new global economy, and indeed, it was. It was a huge realigning for the economy and for the "corporation" families.

Oh there were the usual polite, vanilla responses of. "We'll look into it." But for all their protesting and letter writing, it didn't make one bit of difference. They all got "RIFed" anyway. The scene of the "slippery slope" was not lost on me. I could see it coming, and it didn't look pretty.

The manager of Jerry's division called them in for a meeting one morning and gave them all a copy of the now-famous book, *Who Moved My Cheese?* He told them that they needed to read it. He said that a lot of big changes were coming, and he thought the book might help prepare them. And that really was about all he had to say about that. I read Jerry's book aloud at home. He's a "techie" guy, so he didn't really understand the subtle message. But I did. I knew there was a bad moon on the rise somewhere in our not-too-distant future.

Not long after that, the RIFs came fast and hard. I referred to them as "corporate executions." Since Jerry was an IT manager, he got the "execution list" because his department was charged with shutting down the technology access and erasing the terminated employees from the system. He would usually get the list on Wednesday or Thursday, and the following day, the named employees would be "RIFed" and escorted from the building, and Jerry would erase them from the computer system—just like they never existed. It was brutal on his psyche.

He began to withdraw emotionally. He was never really a big talker anyway. He usually tossed and turned the night before the "corporate execution," talking about the people on the execution list. As a twenty-six-year employee, he knew most of them, their families, and their circumstances. I'm sure that equally disturbing for him was the haunting task of waiting for his own turn—the one that he knew would come. I hated them for what they were doing to people, especially my husband. The remaining employees began to refer to each other in death terms. Those not on the list were called "survivors."

Jerry's turn came in the middle of the week, on a Wednesday, in 2002. He was working from home by then. The Corporation was saving money by asking everyone to work from home. The social isolation had not been good for Jerry. But the pay and benefits were still good, so he stayed and dreamed of the day he could retire and fish. That fateful February morning, around eleven o'clock, he called and asked me to come home. He said that several of them had been noticed for a conference call at one o'clock. He knew the drill all too well.

I held his cool, clammy hand and waited for the call. He asked me to listen in from another phone. Jerry dialed in for the call, and the "executioner" came on the line. He was brief and to the point: "As you all know, we've had a downturn in business, so we're having an RIF, and you all are on that list. We appreciate your service. Your benefits expire at midnight tonight. Bring your computers in to HR tomorrow, and they will go over COBRA and any other questions you may have. I'll turn the call over to HR now."

It was swift and stunning. The corporate executions do not come with instructions or time for preparations. They hurl you into shock and leave you in the place I call *Bottom Side Up*—a place where nothing is the same.

At midnight, we were lying in bed, still awake but silent as the clock chimed twelve times. The insurance was gone. The job was gone. We were no longer a Corporate family. Our life had turned *Bottom Side Up*, and that moment marked our descent down the economic ladder and ended our ideal of the American dream. Mama called those kinds of things "an early frost."

Bottom Side Up was disorienting. I felt queasy and terribly uncomfortable. It reminded me of getting stuck upside down on a malfunctioning carnival ride, where the damn thing just keeps on going round and round. The view is distorted; you feel disoriented and helpless. The carnival music just keeps on playing like nothing is happening, and nobody notices, except the ones on the ride—the ones who are *Bottom Side Up*.

That night I prayed, although I still held several grudges against the "Big Guy." I tried to make some deals, but I knew from experience that you can't deal your way through anything except politics, and God doesn't make deals anyway. Having lost my only child to teen suicide a decade earlier, I was no stranger to the rain or to arguments with God.

I felt scared, confused, and very alone. Jerry didn't want to talk about it. I tried to tell myself that Jerry would find another job right away, but the image of the engineers with the little American flags on the cubicles haunted me. The good jobs were gone. I knew all too well the meaning of outsourcing. We finally fell into a fitful sleep. I was hoping that we would wake up tomorrow, and it would all just have been a bad dream. I quietly worried about Jerry. He was a loyal "techie" guy, not given to talking about his feelings.

Jerry got up the next morning just like he had done for twenty-six years. He went through his methodical daily ritual of putting on a sock and a shoe...and a sock and a shoe. He picked up his briefcase, ready to go, but today, there was nowhere to go. Little did we know that this scenario would be repeated again and again over the next decade. It would be like the movie *Groundhog Day*. It's a good thing we don't know the future.

We stood by the coffee pot, holding each other and crying. The coffee pot has always had a way of comforting me. It was what my parents did on the farm. They would pour a cup of coffee and talk about whatever it was that needed to get fixed. Jerry looked at me with the saddest eyes and said, "I don't know what to do." I held him tightly and reassured him as best I could. I told him that he had done nothing wrong. This wasn't his fault, and we would be fine. I never told him, but I didn't know what to do either.

LIFE BEFORE THE CRACK

Jerry and I had married in 1993, and I had relocated from Tennessee to Florida. We lived in a 'commuter community' between Orlando and Daytona Beach. Jerry was from Tennessee too. He had relocated to Florida in the late seventies to work for a very powerful global high-tech manufacturing corporation in their information technology department. Our community was a community of eighty thousand people from somewhere else, and most of them worked outside the county, along the I-4 technology corridor.

The community wasn't even a city until its incorporation in December 1995. It was one of the largest population and landmass areas ever to become incorporated. Nestled between the St. Johns River and the Atlantic Ocean, the cultural hub of Orlando, and the fast cars of Daytona, it seemed like an ideal place to live.

When I moved to Florida, I quickly blended into the community, becoming part of the corporate-commuter-family culture. I had a strong and successful background in health care and government relations. For a while, I kept a few of my clients in Tennessee. But I was offered a "too-good-to-turn-down job," working as a Field Coordinator of Business and Government Relations for a very successful national home-health-care agency.

Like everyone else in the community, I worked somewhere else and traveled frequently. That's why they called it a bedroom community. We only came home to sleep. I read the local paper every day, but it seemed strange not to know anyone personally. Jerry and I took long weekend trips and boated on the St. Johns River. I loved the fresh shrimp, crab legs, and lobster. Life was good, except I missed Tennessee and Mama. I longed for the kind of personal and community intimacy I had known in Tennessee. I loved being part of a community and working on community initiatives. I loved engaging people and solving community problems through public policy. I also loved the kind of community where everybody knew your name. I had a strong need to "belong." But here in the bedroom community, nobody knows anybody's name. It was kind of sad. I tried not to think about it much. I joined the local Chamber of Commerce, seeking a connection to the community.

By 1994, the health-care system was becoming strained. We all knew the Medicare system was fragile and coming under tougher regulations. Our company, which was the largest privately held home-care agency in the nation, had come under regulatory scrutiny. I was becoming increasingly disillusioned with the health-care system in general. Going to work every morning no longer made me happy. I was negotiating contracts that required me to sharpen my pencil so much that I didn't think our agency could provide decent care for what we were being paid. (Sometime you reach a point where you can't do more with less.) I wasn't interested in providing any other kind of health care except the best. I was becoming restless. I wanted something different, something more, and something with meaning. Looking back, I now realize that surviving the death of a child will force you on a lifelong journey in search of meaning, whether you want to go or not.

We had gone to California for my birthday in July of 1995. (My life seems to always turn *Bottom Side Up* in July.) On the flight back, staring out into the clouds, I decided I was going to resign from the health-care agency. Jerry thought that I was crazy.

"What are you going to do?" he asked.

Staring out the airplane window, I just simply said, "I don't know." I was spoiled by Jerry's job. We had good health-care benefits, and I lived pretty simply anyway. Things or money never really made me happy. I loved people and projects with meaning, simplicity, and traveling. I absolutely did love traveling. That's what I wanted to do when we retired.

Returning to work the following week, I gave a thirty-day notice and walked away. Less than a year later, the CEO and his wife were indicted for Medicare fraud. They were later convicted, and the agency closed. I was grateful that I had escaped the stress and humiliation of representing a company while the CEO was being indicted. After leaving the health-care company, I went back to working for myself again, picking up short term projects. I had no idea what I wanted to do. The healthcare system was not a place I wanted to be anymore.

I volunteered some time with the local chamber of commerce. They were working on a huge community initiative to incorporate the community, and the project excited me. It was cool to run different financial scenarios and to plan out a city. Who gets to do that in their lifetime? At the Chamber, I made friends easily and found the connections I was craving. The community was polarized by the incorporation issue. This was the third incorporation attempt. The referendum finally passed in November 1995. On December 31, 1995, the community officially became a municipality.

Three very visionary gentlemen and I were hired as consultants to get the city up and running. The project was exciting, and I was happy. They called us the "Dream Team." Our office was three small rooms in a strip shopping mall, which we quickly transformed into the city hall. We had no paper, no paper clips—nothing except the vision and the mandate of sixty-eight thousand citizens who wanted a city. I was assuming that they, like me, longed for community intimacy and a relationship with their elected leaders. I did not take their vision lightly. I wanted to know their names as much as they wanted to know mine. Riding in our first parade, I cried when I saw the citizens on the side of the road waving at us. They were depending on us for their future. I hoped we were everything they had hoped we would be, and I hoped that we could build the kind of city and community that would be worth having—a place where they would be proud to raise their families.

My project lasted for three years. I became an employee of the city and served as interim city manager for almost a year while the City was searching for a permanent manager. During those three years, we expanded quickly, moving from the three rooms to a larger building, and began planning the construction of a city hall. Since we had no Commission Chambers, I carried a box with me, labeled "Portable City Hall." Its contents: a gavel and the nameplates of all the commissioners. We met wherever we could.

Bottom Side Up

It seemed beautifully simplistic to me: just us, the box, and the people. The Fire Chief and I pulled desks and chairs out of a college warehouse. Sometimes we had to empty out a drawer full of rats or roaches. We were running the austerity plan, just like the citizens said they wanted. They did not give the new city the authority to bond, so we were on a pay-as-you-go plan. I was comfortable with it. It was the way we did it on the farm. It turned out that the citizens were right, and that early austerity probably saved the city during the economic meltdown of 2009, when property values dropped by 60 percent and were among the top foreclosure locations in the nation.

We held public meetings anywhere we could get a table and space enough for the residents (just us, the box, and the people). I later began to hire more staff. The first one was a beautiful sassy black woman named Helen. I loved her the first time I met her. She was smart and had the greatest sense of humor and more shoes than anyone I knew. I did not know it the day I hired her, but she would become one of the "touchstones" in my life.

While creating a city was exciting, we had also created a bureaucracy, and I was beginning to feel isolated from the community. From the incorporation study, I knew the city could not financially survive on a residential tax base. We had to bring in economic development to diversify the tax base. So after a permanent manager was hired, I left the city in 1999 to run the local Chamber of Commerce. It was the love-of-my-life job—a place where I finally found the community intimacy I craved.

And that was where I was when the tech bubble burst, Jerry lost his big corporate job, and we first turned *Bottom Side Up*. I wasn't really concerned about my job—after all, every community had a chamber of commerce. We had resigned ourselves to the fact that Jerry would never make the kind of money that he had made at his big job. What we did not know was that jobs in the technology industry were virtually nonexistent. How could that be possible, here in the high-tech corridor in the shadow of the "Big Mouse?"

2003

Jerry eventually got a job selling boats. His salary was nothing compared to what he made at the Corporation. But oddly enough, Jerry seemed happy. Besides computers, his other love was boats. Part of our retirement dream was to buy a houseboat and meander up and down the St. Johns River, the one that runs north.

Jerry began to smile and talk again, and he seemed to have gotten over the shock of having lost his 'big job'. I had managed for the Chamber to be able to participate in a group health-care plan, and so Jerry was now covered under my plan. The boat store owner was getting up in years and looking to sell the store. We almost bought it, but our financial manager asked Jerry if perhaps he was just trying to buy himself a job. It was such a revealing question. The next day we declined the boat store offer. Looking back, that was the best decision we ever made. About a month later, Jerry lost his job again.

The second blow wasn't quite as hard as the first one. The salary was nothing, and there were no benefits. He mostly was sad that he lost his fun job. It's strange how entangled we become with our jobs.

Bottom Side Up

He consulted for a couple of years, picking up a project every now and then. After a couple of years, he got another low-paying help-desk job in the IT department of a nonprofit mental health center. He was amazed at the lack of urgency in the nonprofit world, compared to the global speed of his prior job. At least here he had some benefits and health insurance. Jerry had been diagnosed with type 2 diabetes a few years earlier, so health insurance was a really big deal for us—as it is for most Americans. We had adjusted fairly well to the lower-paying jobs.

My conservative survival instincts from the farm kicked in, and we started planning for a rainy day. It looked to me like the storm clouds were already gathering. We sold our rental house and paid off our mortgage. We never lived extravagantly anyway. We were saving our money for that houseboat and trips to faraway places. I was hoping for a summer house in Tennessee.

Mama was the only close family I had left, and I wanted to spend more time with her again. She was my best friend, and I still missed her terribly, even though we talked on the phone every day. I kept my worries to myself, except for sharing them with Mama. She could always make me feel better with her simple, slow-talkin' Tennessee wisdom.

Slowly, those dreams of a Tennessee summer house and a houseboat seemed to fade into one big blur. I tried not to think about it. All in all, we had gotten back up to sideways—which was better than *Bottom Side Up*, in case you're wondering.

Life was still good at the Chamber. I practiced gratitude every day, writing in my gratitude journal. Sometimes, I was just simply grateful for a cup of coffee and a phone call from Mama.

> *I could see within and without.*
> —THE GREAT GATSBY

As I mentioned, our community was a commuter community, located in the I-4 high-tech corridor. When the technology bubble burst, it ripped silent but gaping wounds in the very fabric of the community. But it was a disconnected bedroom community, and no one really noticed—except at the Chamber. Things were really busy for us.

All the techies who had lost jobs in the tech meltdown were coming to us for business counseling, trying to set up their own consulting companies. Inside the Chamber, the buzz was about what had happened to the tech industry. No one else talked about it much, but we certainly realized that technology jobs were being outsourced to India and other places, and that could not be good. It seemed like a very bad moon on the rise, but no one else much noticed.

I complained to public officials every chance I got, but no one seemed alarmed. It was, they said, a natural evolution of a global economy.

The Chamber of Commerce was busier than ever. It seemed like we were trying to save the American dream by helping people start small businesses. By 2001, I had somehow managed to merge three small chambers and survive. Now we finally had a decent-sized chamber representing the business community in three cities. We relocated the merged chamber offices to the regional business hub. Our office was located almost at the entrance of a beautiful state park, home of the endangered Florida manatee. I was busy and happy. Mama said that I worked too much.

Looking back, I guess I was part of the "in" crowd, the ones who know everything and influence decisions for other people. But being the people lover that I am, I just saw the opportunity to ask people what they wanted and then try to make that happen. I wanted to build a community full of American dreams. Just like when I was starting the city, I wanted to create the kind of city that the people wanted. Now I was trying to create the kind of community and quality of life that would nurture the families that were living here.

The new city, once a retirement community and now a commuter community, had over twenty thousand children under the age of eighteen. The once-sprawling rural, unincorporated area was now governed by three cities, two of which had been incorporated in the midnineties. The area was buzzing with housing and commercial development. I was still holding out hope for creating high-value jobs and building a world-class community. My weeks were always sixty-hour weeks, but I talked to Mama almost every day. She always said she missed me and asked when I was coming home.

My days were busy, filled with ribbon cuttings, funerals, public meetings, disaster training, community initiatives, and white-tablecloth (at least three-fork) dinners and banquets, not to mention the administrative tasks of running a nonprofit organization and managing a board of directors. My wardrobe was a portfolio of business suits and cocktail dresses, blue jeans, and polo shirts featuring the Chamber of Commerce pineapple logo. Of course, the staple accessory was the gold-plated Chamber of Commerce name pin, complete with pineapple logo. Every ounce of me was entangled in this job. I lived and breathed the community and the Chamber of Commerce. As I said before, it's strange how our lives become so entangled with our jobs.

I lived for the community and the job. The job was my family. I was my job. My job was me. What I didn't understand then became clearer, looking backward. We were no longer just coming here to central Florida to retire, play golf, die, and be shipped back home for burial. We were coming here to live, to raise families, to watch our children sing and dance and graduate, to work, and to play in the Florida sun.

We had done a decent job of building parks with playgrounds, but clearly, the community wanted more. There were no community centers or gathering places—no place to have black-tie fundraisers like other communities. There was no gathering place in our community to watch our children graduate or to develop a philanthropic culture or to watch our incredibly talented children share their gifts. We were living in a cultural void. The community, now feeling betrayed by the high-tech corporate world, wanted to go home. They wanted to belong. They were desperately seeking some kind of connection to this bedroom community we called home.

I recognized it, because I felt it too. I wanted to call this place home, but I needed something to hold on to. We needed something to glue us together. We had built governments and beauracracies and some commercial establishments. It was now time to build a community culture, to anchor people in community pride, to finally build a place where we could celebrate ourselves.

I was then—and still am today—convinced that community pride is a far more effective tool in creating great neighborhoods than code enforcement. Communities with a strong sense of pride don't need much code enforcement. I was bothered by the fact that, here, we were beginning to use police officers to tell people that their grass needed to be mowed. It just seemed that we were using the wrong tools. You know when you start being a hammer that everything looks like a nail.

The government was acting like young parents who don't really have adequate parenting skills: they tend to use a belt to make their children behave. The other distressing trend was that local nonprofits were coming to increasingly rely more on government subsidy. The root cause, which was not apparent to others but was clearly apparent to me, was simply that we had no corporate partners because we had no corporate businesses. Our county's largest employment sector was the government (HAL), which would later become more problematic than we knew.

More significantly, we had no gathering place large enough to hold fundraising events, which ultimately led to nonprofits and community organizations relying on government to fund operations.

Because we had no indoor spaces, every event we organized had to be hosted outdoors, which was much more labor intensive and expensive. Government codes required police and medical personnel at each event, and since we were parking in fields instead of parking lots, traffic and parking was a nightmare, creating another level of expense and stress for the already-over-stressed nonprofit volunteers. An afternoon downpour, common in Florida, could wipe out a whole fundraising event, causing havoc for a nonprofit budget.

It seemed as though I was always watching the community from "without and within." One day, while overseeing another outdoor event setup, I became keenly aware (probably because I was so exhausted from dragging damn boxes across a field) of how hard it was to function in this community.

The scene in front of me played out like a bad movie: a pickup truck arrived in the field, spinning sand everywhere, followed by a minivan full of wide-eyed children—all dancers.

Women drove the pickup, Moms of the children, I supposed. They all moved toward the back of the pickup, letting the tailgate down to reveal several sheets of plywood. They awkwardly lifted the plywood and, with great effort, lugged one sheet at a time to a nearby grassy area, which we had spray-painted and numbered earlier, indicating their space in the field. This would be the place where the dancing children would later perform.

Another larger caravan, driven mostly by men, was arriving. These were the people who would build and assemble the stage. That was followed by the food trucks and then the community organizations—all dragging a tent and a table. The table drapes had to be taped down for protection against the wind. The tent, of course, was for protection from the harsh Florida sun and the usual afternoon rain. An awesome community leader (and also a Vietnam veteran) owned the communication radios and always lent his logistical talents to assist with the very complicated setup.

If Lady Luck was with us, it wouldn't rain, and someone would bring a camper that we could use in order to rest a few minutes out of the sun and perhaps wash our faces. I thought it looked like a damn wagon train going through the desert—except that we weren't in search of a better place; we actually lived here. It was excruciating and complex.

I wondered how long we could keep it up. Mostly I wondered why we settled for this. But somehow, time after time, we would pull it all together, and the show would begin. The audience would show up, carrying their own chairs, hoping to find a nice shade tree. Some who didn't have time to pack a chair—usually the proud parents of the children performers—would sit on the hot bleachers, basking in the pride of nurturing these magnificent children. And they were magnificent. When they went to the plywood and began to dance, it would take my breath away. On that particular day, I made my mind up to do something better. Why couldn't we build something with a roof and an air conditioner and a stage that didn't have to be brought in on a truck? Why couldn't we dress up and sell dinner tickets and promote philanthropic efforts like the progressive communities—especially those who had an abundance of talented children and willing parents.

Soon after, I made an impassioned speech at one of our chamber events, challenging our community: "Every day we incubate something. Are we incubating dancers and artists or gang members? Are we incubating creative communities or stagnant beauracracies? Are we incubating prosperity or poverty? Are we finding solutions or creating problems? There is no way around it, every day we incubate one thing or the other." It was one of my finer public speeches. (At least I thought so.)

Within a few months of this speech, I was excited to be spearheading one of the largest projects that had ever been attempted in our community. The community was finally going to get a gathering place. We would finally become real. The project was incredibly complex, pulling together at least seven funding sources: three cities, a college, the county, the state of Florida, and the chamber of commerce. Somehow, I had come to be the glue holding a thirty-million-dollar multipurpose community center construction project together. It was a *big* project! We named it the "Partnership Project."

Back at home, Jerry was sad and lost without his corporate job. He didn't smile very much anymore. But I was really too busy to worry about it. Jerry was pretty low maintenance, and he never talked about how he felt anyway. When we were dating and started getting serious and he had brought up the subject of my perhaps moving to Florida, I had invited him to come to Washington, where I was lobbying. I told him I wanted him to see how I worked before he had thoughts about getting serious. It apparently didn't bother him. He had proposed to me on the steps of the Capitol, where I was sitting, barefoot, in my business suit, watching the sun go down. He had always supported me in anything I had wanted to do.

I knew he was depressed about losing his job and his identity, but he didn't want to talk about it.

That's the way he rolled. Being a techie, he thinks everything has a technical solution. I didn't think this one did, which was probably why he didn't want to talk about it.

Politically, I was very angry and concerned about the trend of outsourcing American jobs overseas. That made me all the more committed to the American dream and my Chamber of Commerce. I loved the little guys—the entrepreneurial spirits, main street, and community banks. I was my job. Every day when I woke up, I couldn't wait to get to work. I was so excited to be working on the Partnership Project. It was crazy, but I felt lucky.

2004

It was on a Saturday, just a couple of days before my birthday in 2004. It seems like all the bad things always happen right around my birthday, which, by the way, I mentioned is in July.

Mama hadn't seemed like herself lately. She had not answered the phone on Friday night when I had called. I had just assumed that she was feeling better and had gone out with one of her friends.

That Saturday morning, I called again, and when she answered the phone, I knew something was terribly wrong. She yelled at me for calling her so much and told me to leave her alone. I told her I was sorry to bother her, and that I would let her rest. I hung up the phone and quickly called my aunt. I told her to hurry over and check on Mama—that I just knew something was "bad wrong." (That's Tennessee country talk for a crisis, in case you're wondering. When you tell Tennessee people to "come quick, something's bad wrong" they get there in a hurry.) Within a half hour, Mama was being transported by ambulance to a regional hospital in critical condition and not expected to live.

A rare and aggressive tumor had broken through her chest wall. She had lost a lot of blood, but she was still conscious. She confided in my aunt that she was mad at me for calling her. She had just wanted to die in peace and not bother anybody. That was the stubborn Mama I loved (and where I get most of my stubbornness from). I quickly booked the next flight to Tennessee to be at her side. I would fly into Nashville, get a rental car, and then drive two-and-a-half hours to the hospital. I promised her when I moved to Florida that I would always come home if she needed me. Today, I was being asked to make good on that promise.

The next day was my birthday. Mama was clinging to life with a 104-degree temperature. Instinctively, I climbed into the hospital bed beside her. As I lay holding her, it dawned on me that we were in the same hospital where I was born, the place where she sang "Amazing Grace" as I was being born. That night, I held her in my arms and softly sang "Amazing Grace" to her. I hoped it comforted her. I laughed and told her we hadn't come very far.

Mama was a very religious woman. Her pastor came that night and asked God to have mercy on her soul and forgive her sins and then implied that this illness was punishment for something she had done. The prayer pissed me off. I wanted him to say something else. I wanted him to tell her that she was a wonderful woman, and that God sure loved her. I wanted her pastor to comfort her. I wanted her God to be sorry that she was sick. And I wanted her pastor to tell her that she was going to be just fine. But he didn't.

A big knot was forming in my stomach. Somehow, I mustered the courage to ask him to leave. Mama was too sick to notice, and for that, I was grateful. She would have been very mad at me. I was going to have a little talk with God, and like Daddy used to say, I did not need a middleman. The pastor looked at me like I was a heathen. He leaned over Mama and told her to let him know if she needed anything. He left without acknowledging or saying good-bye to me.

After he was gone, I shut the door and crawled back in bed with her. I wrapped my arms around her fever-ravished body and held her fiercely. She told me that she loved me, and she thought the Lord would take her away that night, to which I replied, "Well, Mama, if He comes tonight, He's going to have to kick my ass to get you. I'm not letting you go."

Even through her fever, she scolded me. "Linda, don't talk that way about God."

Knowing that I had offended her and possibly God, I just lovingly but fiercely held her. She told me to "hush up," and I did because I was way more afraid of Mama than I was of God. In my irreverent and loving arms, she drifted off in a quiet and peaceful sleep while I held her and stood my ground with God all night.

I was thinking that if she lived and found out I had asked the preacher to leave because I didn't like his prayer, she was really going to be mad at me. But I wanted her to know how incredible she had been. I wanted the prayers said over her to be gentle and comforting. And mostly, I wanted her to know that she had never done anything to cause this terrible illness to be visited upon her. And when she woke up, I was going to tell her just that very thing: that I no longer believed (actually I had not believed in many years) that God gets up every day, boots up His computer, and decides who needs to be punished that day. He doesn't even have an app for that anyway. I wasn't even sure what God's role was in all of this. To tell the truth, I wasn't sure who was in charge of this whole thing—whatever this "whole thing" is.

As the hours passed and night turned into day, I wondered how I would keep my promise to always be there for her. I had this huge project going on in Florida, which tonight seemed so far away. But like Scarlett O'Hara in *Gone with the Wind*, I decided to think about that tomorrow.

As dawn broke, so did Mama's fever. We had won the battle, but I knew the war was just beginning. Waking from her feverish sleep, she looked up at me, smiled, and asked "You been right here all night?"

Smiling back at her, I replied, "Well, good morning, and yes, as a matter of fact, I have been right here all night."

She said, "Looks like you won."

I hugged her and smiled. "Damn skippy, I did." She quickly admonished me for "cussing," and I knew she was better.

Bottom Side Up

When the doctor came in, he said to her, "Well, Miss Dorothy, you look pretty good this morning. What happened?"

She nodded toward me and said, "Ask her."

I told him the story about God having to kick my ass to take her. He let out a big belly laugh and hugged me hard. His hug was so strong and reassuring. He looked me straight in the eye, and for a fleeting moment, I thought maybe he might be God.

Mama apologized for me and told him she didn't raise me to talk like that. "But I do feel better. Maybe she did scare Him off."

I stayed at the hospital thirteen days and nights, running the Chamber from my laptop and a cell phone. I had to sit in the window to get cell-phone coverage. Some days I wore the same clothes two days in a row, but I kept Him scared off for another eighteen months.

Over the course of that time, life would ask me to choose between keeping my promise to always be there for Mama or to run this epic project for the Chamber of Commerce. For a while, I tried to do both. My tools were Southwest Airlines, a laptop, a cell phone, and a "go bag." I was an only child, so there wasn't anybody else to turn to.

Mama had a brother and a sister. They could help, but still, she was my responsibility and my promise. Mostly, she was my Mama, and I loved her and wanted to be with her every moment I could.

I came to love Southwest Airlines. They were always on time and cheerful. God knows I needed cheerful. And we had a schedule that worked like clockwork. I flew back and forth every week, managing the Chamber, the Partnership Project, my house, Mama's house, and her illness, which was complicated by a staph infection and chemo. I was exhausted.

That was 2004 and the worst hurricane season in years. Florida had three hurricanes right in our community. The electricity was out for a week on two occasions. I traveled between the crises of weather and chemo.

One night, I was facilitating my annual Chamber of Commerce leadership class retreat on the beach when I got a call from Mama's physician. He informed me that Mama had suddenly become very ill, and he was putting her in ICU. I had to find someone to take over the class that night and sometime around midnight, I made the usual flight to Nashville, which entailed picking up a rental car and making the 2 1/2 hour drive to the hospital.

Exhausted and frazzled, I drank wine on the plane and cried. A guy sitting next to me asked me if I had just broken up with somebody and I said "yes, as amatter of fact I think I have. I think I'm breaking up with my life." He asked me what was wrong. Between sniffles, I shared that I was just really tired, and that my life was just so damn *Bottom Side Up*. I think he realized that it was better to let it be. He closed his eyes as if trying to sleep. It looked like a great idea to me too. It would probably be the last sleep I would get for days. I finished my wine and lay my head into the window, watching the clouds go by.

That night; streaks of lightning were illuminating the clouds in the most spectacular fireworks show. The scene was surreal, or perhaps I was just exhausted. I wondered if there really was a heaven, and did God really live up here, and why did He allow so much pain in the world— and especially to me. I picked up the rental car in Nashville and drove the two-and-a-half hours to the hospital in a dense fog. It seemed as if I was the only person left on earth.

Exhausted, I arrived around 3:00 a.m. at the hospital. I knew it was against hospital rules to allow me into the ICU at that time. But you must know by now that I tilt at windmills, and yes, they let me into her room.

"You're here," she smiled weakly. "I'm sorry I got sick again."

"It's okay. I'm here, and they're taking good care of you. That's all that matters."

"Are you staying here tonight?"

"Caressing her head, I answered, "I am. I'll be here when you wake up."

"I love you," she whispered.

"I love you too, Mama."

Bottom Side Up

Autumn came to me in two different worlds: Florida, still cleaning up from three devastating hurricanes, and Tennessee, brilliantly dressed in the fall colors that I loved. Mama was still going through chemo, and I had 'round-the-clock care with her. I called three times a day and went home at least every two weeks. She was stable, but the battle was fierce.

On one of my trips home, I tried to get Mama to let me start packing away some of her things. She had a collection of angels and rabbits. Secretly, I had hoped we could start with the rabbits. Mentally, I was preparing for her eventual death. Smart woman that she was, she picked right up on it.

"No, Linda we're not doing anything with all this stuff right now. I can just hear you now. When I die, you'll bury me and then walk in here, put your hands on your hips, and say, 'What the hell am I going to do with all this stuff?' So just move along off that subject. You can worry with that later—after I'm gone."

She was so very right. That's exactly the way it went down.

Back at the Chamber, the Partnership Project was in full swing. I had hired a consultant from Salt Lake City to help the Chamber with the capital campaign to raise two million dollars.

I had an awesome staff, which I empowered to run the Chamber. I was mostly focused on the project, community relations, taking care of my Board, my Florida family, and Mama.

However, the stress of the project was beginning to weigh heavily on me: business suits for Florida—blue jeans for Tennessee. I lived with my feet firmly planted in two worlds. I learned to be fully attentive and present in whatever world I was living in that day. It was the only way I could survive. I had trimmed my "big life" down to just the essentials of a "go bag." I managed organizational meetings of the partners for the project and chemo and caregiver schedules for Mama. I managed nothing for me. Jerry supported me any way that he could. But the stress was hard on us both.

Life became a tapestry of small things and large things: a bowl of Cheerios, a blood clot, clean panties, a thirty-million-dollar deal, a go bag, a legacy project, the joy of eating ice cream with Mama, a luncheon at the country club. I was, moment by moment, like someone on a teeter-totter, falling one moment toward death and the next moment falling toward life. I felt as if I were on some driverless train.

2005

They say that time changes everything, but you actually have to change it yourself.

—ANDY WARHOL

My friend Sage had lost the 2004 election in November that year. I had been offered a job as public information officer and community relations director for a nearby city—the city where the Partnership Project would be built.

I knew that Mama's illness was too aggressive for her to survive. And I knew that any day now, I might have to go to Tennessee for an extended period. The project was much too critical to leave unattended. I was worried about how to handle it all. My life was messy. The thought came to me that Sage could take over the Chamber, and I would go to the city. I kept that thought in my mind, especially as I became more exhausted. I was slowly realizing that I could no longer do justice to anything—the Chamber, Mama, or myself. I finally broached the subject with Sage. Surprisingly, she said yes.

In December of that year, exhausted and broken open, I resigned my chamber job. I was optimistic that this scenario could work for all of us. I could go to a less stressful schedule at the city, and Sage could come to work at the chamber. She loved the Chamber, and she loved big projects. The Partnership Project was as big and complex as it gets. She still had enough residual political power to raise money for the capital campaign. Sage questioned why I would leave the Chamber when I loved this project so much.

It was true—I was in love with this project, but I was also in love with this amazing human being, my mother—one thing trying to be born; the other, trying to die. I was caught in the middle. The stress was overwhelming.

Sage was the only one I knew to be capable of moving this thirty-million-dollar-community Partnership Project through. Working with six partners plus the Chamber and the private sector was no easy task. Plus, I thought that since she was my best friend and loved the Chamber, she would take care of my staff as well as the project and the organization. Sage had a vibrant energy about her, and she loved talking to people and being on the phone. People don't believe me, but I am an introvert. Letting her cut the ribbon and take all the credit for the project was not a problem for me. I didn't care. I just wanted this audacious project to be finished so that our children could sing and dance, and the community could learn and gather together for fundraisers and black-tie dinners and art shows and farmers markets. I figured that I had made the best decisions for everyone under some tough circumstances.

So in January, I took my place in the city government, and Sage took her place at the Chamber of Commerce. Life was strange. I felt like I was on the outside looking in. In March, a group of us made our annual lobby trip to Tallahassee during the legislative session. That year, we were putting on the ritz in the top floor of the Florida state capitol with our "Around the World" legislative reception. Legislators and "suits" tasted decadent desserts, coffees, and liquors representing countries all over the world. I found myself sitting on the windowsill of the State Capitol, with a cup of coffee, watching from "without and within." I was comfortable in the window.

I had gotten used to sitting in the windowsill of Mama's hospital room, mostly because I could get a phone signal there. And suddenly, I felt so out of place. It all seemed so shallow and pretentious. Sitting in this window overlooking the seat of power, I felt like a fake—like a person assigned a role in a play. I never felt that way in the hospital window.

The County Chairman came over to the window and sat down by me. We engaged in real conversation. He told me that he was tired and shared some of the hateful political antics that were swirling around us. He told me about his little grandson and how he made him smile. I told him about Mama and why I had changed jobs. We talked for so long that his staff came over and reminded him to "work the room." Standing, almost embarrassed because he had lost track of time, he graciously said, "Thank you for the conversation."

"Ditto."

He went about his business, and I drank another glass of champagne, sitting in the window, watching from "without and within."

"People change and forget to tell each other."
—LILLIAN HELLMAN

The trade was not a good fit for either Sage or me. In hindsight, it only worked in my exhausted mind and in her grief from losing an election. But we were where we were. I was grateful to be working around a great bunch of people at the city, and I was still flying back and forth to care for Mama, although she was doing a little better. She had even gone back to work part time, where she was director of Meals on Wheels, even though she was still getting radiation every day.

Occasionally, I could go three weeks without flying home.

Back at the Chamber, Sage was quickly making changes that surprised me. She fired, I think it was actually labeled as an RIF (I hate that word), one of my long-standing employees, the gentle one with the twins—the one I promised I would never make feel guilty if she had to take off work for the children. I was devastated. Sage wrote a big bunch of new rules. I've never been too big on rules. Heartfelt leadership is more my style. Heartfelt leadership is pretty simple and a lot less expensive to implement and manage. Not one of my team members was ever afraid to a make a decision. I raised 'em that way on purpose.

I could begin to sense that she didn't really love what I had loved after all, including the Partnership Project. I was rocked with guilt for letting down the partners and the community who needed a gathering place and the children who needed a place to sing and dance. I was beginning to feel betrayed by my best friend. I didn't much like how it felt. Sometimes I wondered if you could ever really have a best friend who was a politician. But Mama was too sick, and I was so busy with city government business and taking care of Mama that I just didn't have the strength to worry about it.

Mama had a good spring. I drove her the first day she returned to work like a mother who would drive her child to the first day of school. She was wearing a yellow blouse and white pants. I watched her until she disappeared behind the door of the old red-brick elementary school, now a senior meal site, where she managed the senior meal program and the place where they adored her and called her "Miss Dorothy." She was feisty. The people loved her there, and for a few months, she blossomed in their love. But by the end of summer, the tumor had returned with vengeance.

In early August, Mama surprisingly told me that she wanted to come to Florida for a few weeks. She wanted to get away from everybody telling her what to do. She thought she would enjoy looking out at the lake with me in the morning. Maybe, she said, she would even stay through the winter. I found it ironic that she wanted to sit in my oak swing and look out over the lake from my Florida room. Here was my favorite place in the world—the place where I returned over and over again to find myself. That lake had comforted us through so many of our life's ups and downs.

We quickly made preparations to bring Mama to Florida. Mama didn't learn to drive until after Daddy had passed away. She loved her car more than just about anything, and she said there was only one condition about coming to Florida—that she needed to have her car. So, being the "fixer of all things" that I was, Jerry and I flew up to Tennessee and drove Mama and her car back to Florida. She rested in the back seat.

I was in the front seat on the phone, giving media briefings about a bank robbery that had occurred back in the city where I was working as the public information officer. No one from the media ever knew that I was in a car driving across three states, bringing my mother to my home to die. It seemed like a strange thing to be doing, but Mama and I talked about the robbery between her naps. It seemed to take our minds off of the sad reality of what we both knew was her final journey. Things are sometimes that way in *Bottom Side Up*.

Arriving back at home, I was consumed with the details of getting Mama settled in. We live in a two-story house. My good man, Jerry, took the upstairs bedroom so that I could put Mama in our bedroom. I paid attention to every detail that could make her comfortable. That was from years of doing home health care and organizing events for the Chamber. I wanted everything to be perfect. Every banquet hall in the area knew that "Ms. White likes the salads preset for her events."

Sage came over and brought a box of assorted desserts from our favorite restaurant when Mama first arrived. Later, she asked me why I would take on such a huge responsibility of caring for my mother in her last days.

"Because it's who I am. If you don't understand, I probably can't explain. I can't save her, but I can make her last days loving and peaceful. It's just the way I roll." My father had died in my arms, and his father had died at home in his arms. I was raised to believe that death is a part of life—one of the more difficult parts, I might add.

Don't surrender your loneliness, let it cut more deep.
—HAVIZ

Our last days together were beautiful and bittersweet. Mama told me family secrets. We giggled and cried and held each other's hands. I told her secrets. I put her in my big four-poster bed and slept with her, savoring every last moment. I wanted to remember the way she smelled, the way her skin felt, the way her lip crooked up when she didn't like something. I wanted to feel the rise and fall of her every breath, knowing the moment would come when there was no breath. And mostly, I wanted her in her last moments to feel loved and unafraid. This was my "rite of passage" to a life without a mother.

Being sensitive to her need for a spiritual advisor, I brought everybody I could find to the house to pray with her. We both knew I wasn't good at the kind of praying she thought she needed—you know, the prayer about saving her wretched soul. So I brought in everybody I could find: men, women, black, white, Baptists, Methodists, nondenominational Chaplains, etc. One day, I had a Lutheran minister scheduled to see her. I kept trying to find someone she was really comfortable with.

That morning she asked me, "Well, who you got coming to see me today?"

"A Lutheran minister," I replied as I smiled.

With that crooked lip she made when she didn't like something, she quipped, "Well I don't want no ol' Lutherans praying over me."

"Mama, you don't even know any Lutheran ministers. How could you possibly know that you don't like them?"

Curious, and obviously getting quite comfortable discussing religion with me, she asked why she didn't know any Lutherans.

"Because they drink alcohol, and you live in a dry county in the Bible belt where nobody, especially preachers, admits to drinking."

She said she didn't think preachers should drink, and that I was going to keep on until I got her and me both sent straight to hell. I laughed—but not where she could see me.

Just then, the doorbell rang, and there stood the Lutheran minister. Properly attired, wearing black suit and white clerical collar, he arrived with a gift in hand, which was none other than—you guessed it—a very nice bottle of wine.

"Oh how kind of you, please do come in," I remarked, quickly whisking the bottle of wine from his hand. I whispered to him, "She doesn't believe in drinking. Just don't mention the wine to her.

But thanks," I smiled, "'cause I'm good with it."

He sat with her for the longest time that day, and of all the spiritual advisors she loved the most, it was him—the Lutheran with the wine. He visited her daily while the sand was running out of her hourglass. She said she really loved that he had a white collar. She wondered if Florida was the only place where preachers wore the white collar because she didn't remember ever seeing anybody in Tennessee wearing one.

I smiled—but not where she could see me.

Not many days before the sand ran out of her hourglass, she asked if he was coming over that day, and I nodded yes.

She took my hand and sweetly said, "Linda, I like Lutherans. Maybe one day you could become one. You know I worry a lot about your soul. You could be a Lutheran and still drink your wine. You don't drink that much anyway."

I had hired a CNA to help out with Mama. I still tried to work at least part of most days. The city manager where I worked had recently lost his own mother and, during the month that I cared for Mama, he was the most supportive person I had ever known. He knew how hard it was. I was humbled by such tremendous support from a workplace. It was how I thought life and workplaces ought to be. I thought back to how I had managed people in my workplace.

Perhaps, there *is* karma.

One day, I had put on my business suit and had gone to work for a few hours. Coming home that afternoon, I took off the high heels and the business suit and draped it over the chair next to my big four-poster bed, the one Mama was now sleeping in. I quietly slipped into bed beside her. I wrapped her up in my arms while she slept. Like so many times before, I was grateful for the rise and fall of her breath. I begged God to have mercy on me. The business woman might have conducted press briefings that day, but the little girl inside me was begging God, "Please don't take my Mama."

Final Instructions

In one of her final instructional sessions, Mama summoned me to her bedside to sit and talk. By now her condition had deteriorated, and I had moved her to a hospital bed beside the window—the one where she could see the crepe myrtles blooming and the birds eating from the feeder. I knew this talk was going to be serious.

She held my hand, softly rubbing it back and forth. "Linda, I want you to preach my funeral."

Stunned, I could only ask, "Well, Mama, are you sure about that? What about your preacher?"

"Linda when you talk to God, I'm not scared. You say things to Him that I can't say. You say things that I've never heard anybody say—except for maybe your Daddy. No, I'm sure I want it to be you."

And in the final days of her life, the strong woman who had bossed and nagged and beseeched me to always do more only wanted just for me to be with her, to preach her funeral, to tell her final story, and to negotiate her way into heaven because, after all, she still worried about her wretched soul.

Imagine… Mama, wanting me to get her into heaven. Finally, I had done enough. Finally, I was enough. You know that is true when someone just wants to be with you—nothing more, nothing less.

The Sand Runs Out

In the moment of one's last breath, love is all that remains behind. With hurricane Katrina battering New Orleans, Mama died peacefully in my arms. The night before, the Lutheran minister had been at her bedside; he held my hand while he prayed. After he left, I drank the wine.

As I said before, "Life is like an egg: once it gets broken, it's never the same again."

My husband, Jerry, a quiet man who does the most amazing things, had driven to Tennessee during hurricane Katrina to bring Mama's brother and sister to be at her side. It was more for them than anything else. They needed to be with her to have closure. They were at her side as was my best friend, who was still trying to reconcile the death of her own mother. We said good-bye to Mama by placing a bundle of rosemary from my garden in her hands. Finally, it was over, and I was empty—broken open and empty.

God and I called a truce. I asked for help. This was bigger than I was. With tears streaming down my face, I asked Jerry why he thought God would make me hold my own mother while she died.

Jerry just softly said, "He didn't, Linda. You made your own choices about that—just like you always do. You didn't have to disrupt your life, bring her home, and put her in your bed. You could have sent her to the hospital and let the nurses take care of her. You could have had your big project and gone back home near to the end to bury her. But as you say, that's not the way you roll. God gets out of your way—just like all the rest of us do."

His words silenced me.

We made the long burial sojourn back to Tennessee. Daddy was coming across three counties in a flatbed truck (another story); Mama went home by airplane. It was her first time to fly. I asked the funeral director to make sure that she made the angel flight with the rosemary from my herb garden in her hands.

We drove, aunt and uncle in tow, telling funny stories, laughing and crying, 'cause that's how we roll.

Digging up Daddy

Daddy had passed on several years earlier. He had been buried in a cemetery not far from the farm where I had been raised and where he and Mama had toiled day after day, side by side—the place where I am sure Mama embroidered "Mr." and "Mrs." on all her pillowcases and stared into the flames of a fireplace, dreaming of a better life. Farm life can be very hard and lonely.

Mama had always hated that Daddy had chosen the family burial plots in that cemetery. But a woman who embroiders "Mr." and "Mrs." on her pillowcases would never challenge such a decision. Daddy had now been gone more than a decade and, facing her own immortality, she could begin to speak her own truth. Almost every day, in her soft southern drawl, she mentioned how she hated "that cemetery."

One day while we were discussing the situation, I mentioned that she could be buried in the cemetery that she loved. She gasped at me and angrily reminded me of her wifely duties: "Linda, you know full well"—she always used "full well" for emphasis—"that I 'can't *not*' be buried by your daddy. That's my responsibility, and besides, people would talk. My stars—what would the neighbors think?"

And then I offered to fix the problem with what she at first called an "outlandish solution." "Well, we could always move Daddy to the other cemetery."

With glaring eyes, she questioned, "Linda Sue, would you actually dig up your own daddy?"

"Absolutely," I confidently replied. "Mama, he won't mind. He loved you his whole life. All he ever wanted was for us to be happy. He won't mind a bit as long as you're happy."

The whole conversation was weird but we kept having it anyway. Truth telling can sometimes be very strange. She asked me some rather practical questions regarding the logistical process. Then she got a little smile on her face. "You don't think he'll care?"

"No, Mama," I reassured her. "He will be happy as long as you're happy."

She got on the phone to her brother and sister and her very large group of friends and neighbors and announced to them very matter of factly, "Linda is going to dig her daddy up and move him to Lexington Cemetery."

Bottom Side Up

They all quickly showed up to get the details. This was big. Nothing like this had ever happened before that they could remember. So Mama made a big pot of coffee, and somebody brought a pie, and they gathered around the old oak dining table to eat and quiz me about the logistics of "digging up Daddy." They wanted to rest assured that he would be brought across the three counties respectfully in a hearse. Would I have a graveside service? Could they all go?

Funerals and gravesites are very important to Tennessee folks. They schedule complete celebrations around such events. I did not dare tell them the move would most likely be accomplished with a flatbed truck. So I just sweetly said, "No , it will be at night, and they will fix everything up nice and we can all go the next day when it's all fixed up."

Mama and I went to the cemetery, and she picked out their new burial plots. She chose a plot right next to the road and near a shady clump of trees. This time she was in charge. All the logistical details were finished before she came to Florida. Still doubting that the move would really happen, she made me promise that I wouldn't bury her at Lexington Cemetery unless Daddy had gotten there first. I promised.

After the decision was made, Mama briefly wondered out loud what people would think. She always told me it was important that people "think highly of us."

I said, "Well, here's what they'll say. 'Well now, that Miss Dorothy, she does just what she wants.'" It was a dream Mama and many women have had—just to do what they want. It seemed to be a satisfactory end to a hard life. She finally did just what she wanted without worrying about what people thought. The schedule was perfectly timed as if arranged by someone other than me. I was grateful because I certainly wasn't feeling very much in charge. Daddy was coming across three counties on a flatbed truck, and Mama was flying across five states. What was I thinking? I might just wind up going straight to hell for this shenanigan.

Linda S. White

Grace Notes

When I arrived at the funeral home, the matriarch of the local family funeral home greeted me with a reassuring hug. "Oh, honey, I'm so sorry about Miss Dorothy. Your mama sure was a good woman. We're gonna miss her. You doing okay?"

Our small town had two funeral homes owned and operated by local families. The CEOs of both funeral homes were strong women. They had nurtured the town and our family through every tragedy imaginable—always with grace. They were role models for me: compassionate and strong and full of grace.

If I could just get through this funeral, "strong and full of grace."

"Everything worked out perfect; we just got your daddy all situated. I knew you promised your mama." And then, smiling at me, she said, "They sure must love you in Florida. The funeral director in your town put a bundle of rosemary and a note in your Mama's hand that said, 'We love Linda; take good care of her mother.'"

Putting her arm around my shoulder, she gently guided me to her office. She poured me a strong cup of coffee, and we made all the final funeral arrangements. They were not traditional. But the matriarch never blinked an eye.

Replacing the traditional pallbearers, the matriarch of the funeral home and I pushed Mama's sunflower-covered coffin into the chapel, where all our friends and family were gathered for the funeral. As I entered the chapel, I scanned the very full room and caught the eye of my best friend from elementary school. She mouthed to me, "I love you." And I could feel the love in the chapel pushing me forward. The chapel was full—proof of a life well lived.

Mama was a simple woman—not a politician or a philanthropist. But she was obviously loved. And in that moment, I knew that I had been lucky to have been raised by this simply awesome woman. The normal Tennessee funeral song and the one Mama sang the day I was born,

"Amazing Grace," had been replaced by the country song, "The Dance" by Garth Brooks.

The matriarch and I positioned Mama's coffin into place before the empty podium, the place from which I would "preach" her funeral.

I walked over to my stepdaughters, knelt before them, and taking their hands into mine, I whispered, "This is what it means to be a strong woman. We bury each other. We love fiercely, and we write our own stories with courage, compassion and love. I love you." I touched each of my family members, hoping to soak up their love. This was going to be hard. I took a deep breath and stepped to the podium to "preach my mother's funeral."

The journey of pain and the questioning of God had broken me open—broken open like an egg,

broken open enough to let love and courage flow in through the cracks, and broken open enough never to be the same again. Today, I would say good-bye forever to my mother, my advisor, and my best friend. I missed her already. I thanked those who came for loving her and for supporting me. I made a joke about preaching her funeral, and just in case I couldn't get her all the way into heaven, I was asking her preacher to finish up the job with a prayer. But I finally understood what Mama had been trying to teach me all along. Life is too hard, and we are too fragile. You have to believe in "something" bigger than yourself.

At the cemetery, they lowered her casket into the ground, and, picking up a handful of dirt and casting it along with a handful of rose petals on top of her casket as they lowered it into the ground, I gave her back—, keeping only the love she had left behind. And in the end, that's really all that's left of us—whatever love or joy or pain we leave behind. All of us are just on loan anyway.

Walking away, I heard the bells from the First Baptist Church ring three times. A soft September breeze blew over me, and I felt sad but full of grace. I had done well, and, finally, I had become the woman I had always dreamed of being.

Rewind

I felt that I had completed with grace the rite of passage of my mother's death. That was all anyone could hope for. I had no guilt, and I had already done much of my grieving. I had missed the community and the Chamber and the Partnership Center project. I was ready to pick up where I left off. Driving back home to Florida from the funeral, we stopped to pick up a gift for Sage's new granddaughter.

Jerry bought a trailer hitch for her husband's boat. They fished together all the time. I was eager to get my journey of grief behind me. I had done the best that I could for Mama, even under some difficult challenges. I was ready to once again embrace life in the community.

Able to focus on something else besides "Mama and morphine," I began to try to understand what had happened in the community over the past two years. There had been an election, and most of the partners in the "big project" were gone. I hardly knew anyone. (By the way, that's a problem with election term limits.) By all accounts, the election in the largest city (the one I live in) had been a nasty one, and the community had become very polarized.

2006

Just because you don't understand it doesn't mean it isn't so.

—*LEMONY SNICKET,* THE BLANK BOOK

Although I was still working as the public relations and information officer for the city, people began to share with me that things were not going well with the Partnership Project, and that the chamber had become very polarized. The chamber "suits" often invited me to lunch to share that the chamber was not doing well. They really didn't offer specifics, except that the Partnership Project seemed to have lost momentum. When I asked one of the members what he thought the real problem was, he just said, "You're not there."

Sage and I, who used to talk a couple of times a day, hardly ever talked at all anymore. There seemed to be a big elephant between us. In January, she unceremoniously resigned from the chamber and shortly thereafter opened her campaign account to run for a county commission seat—the job she really loved.

Obviously, it wasn't long until the "suits" were pressuring me to take my old job back—the one I really loved.

One day in late March, several of the "suits" invited me to lunch. I was surprised when they talked of things other than the chamber. Over lunch. we laughed like we always did. I thought perhaps they had found someone else to run the Chamber. As we were leaving, one of the "suits" asked me to stop by his car. As he opened his trunk, I spotted a small cooler filled with bags and bags of M&M's (my favorite candy) and several bottles of wine, along with a handwritten sign that simply said, "We love you. Please come back."

And I did.

Going Backward to Move Forward

In May, I made the journey backward. It seemed natural to be back, but the chamber seemed different. There was almost an entirely new staff. I was grateful that Sandy was still there. The new ones were afraid that I would fire them and hire my own, but that's not the way I roll. In fact, one of the new ones particularly delighted me.

Tall and beautiful in a simple kind of way with a North Carolina drawl and a heart the size of Texas, Georgette would become one of my strongest team members. She quickly requested a meeting with me. Straight to the point and looking me straight in the eye, she said, "Ms. White (that's what she called me when she was being serious or sarcastic), if you're gonna fire me, just go ahead and do it and don't be writin' me up and badgerin' me, 'cause that is just going to piss me off."

Holding back a grin, because this was exactly the kind of woman I wanted working for me, I looked her straight in the eye. "Let me tell you something, Ms. Georgette. You have potential. In fact, I think you might be damn near audacious. And here's another thing: the day you come to work for me, your family becomes my family; your pain becomes my pain; your success becomes my success; and your failures become my failures. I am vested in you. I expect only that you do your best every day. Some days, your best will suck, and that's okay. I will empower you to make mistakes and decisions. If things go right, you will get the credit. If things go wrong, I will take the blame. I would also ask that you never kiss my ass or be afraid to tell me that my ideas are bad. However, I would also ask that you be kind when you tell me, for I, too, am human. We are a marketplace of ideas—some good, some bad. But that's the beauty about ideas. I expect that you will work with courage, compassion, and creativity. And don't ever come to work without knowing the price of a gallon of gas, a loaf of bread, and a gallon of milk. They are the stuff of which life is made. Now, go be awesome!"

And she was.

The next gap I filled was with my assistant from my former days at the city, Helen. Helen was very organized, smart, and sophisticated with a wicked sense of humor. I trusted her with my life.

The Chamber and the community were more broken than I had realized. I was going to need a good team to survive the shit storm that I knew was brewing. I began to feel very anxious about the "big project." The partners now looked more like strangers and adversaries. Term limits and an election had washed away many of the thought leaders of the project. That's a real problem with term limits and polarizing politics—as if there are any other kinds anymore.

I was feeling a lot of anxiousness and responsibility. My farming background had instilled in me that a failed project equaled a very bad time—I'm just sayin'.

If the farm crops failed, there was very little for Christmas. There was little of anything until the next season, for that matter. I did not take failure well. I quickly tried to pull the community together for this one defining project. We organized a huge ground-breaking ceremony. The community, all the partners, and news media (including print media and TV) showed up. We brought in a busload of kids to sing and release balloons, signifying the celebrations of their talents that would be showcased in this building. We had an opening date and highlighted the class that would be the first to graduate in this building. It was a sight to behold.

A long string of elected officials from the state all the way down to the locals broke ground with the gold shovels. Surely, they wouldn't kill the project now. Or would they?

As expected, Sage, like me, was also making her journey backward, back into politics. Our journey backward had separated the bonds two friends had made going forward. I knew that if she got back into power, it would be the end of the project—and probably the end of me. So I hurried, anxiously. It was a strange kind of feeling for me to be afraid of the person that used to be the first person I talked to each morning.

But as fate would have it, Sage was returned to elected office in the November election. The morning after the election, I found her campaign sign placed in my parking spot at the chamber. I got a knot in my stomach. It was like finding a horse head in my bed. If I had really known what lay in store for me, I probably would have just quit that day and saved myself a lot of pain. But that's not how I roll.

Heroes and Hypocrites

In a matter of weeks, the "Partnership Project" and I began to be demonized. That's the way politics work. When the politicos don't like a project, they demonize it and its champions. It dies a slow, painful death of a thousand cuts. The champion lets go of the project when he or she is no longer able to fight.

Battered and broken, they crawl out of the ring. I understood the strategy quiet well. But the players surprised me. I would have assumed that anyone could have found enough people that didn't like me to participate in the plot. But the people who assisted in the public flogging just happened to be a few of the members of my local service club, which recently had become more political than humanitarian. Believe me when I tell you that this is never a good thing. Nothing good can come from a humanitarian organization turning political.

> *If at first you don't succeed, try, try again. Then quit.*
> *There's no need in being a damn fool about it.*
> —W. C. FIELDS

The final act came one night at a city commission meeting in the city where I lived—the place where Jerry and I had invested our whole future. Friendly fire is the worst kind of killing.

The "Partnership Project" was on the agenda. There was a newly elected council, and they wanted to undo the funding that had been secured through an inter-local agreement from the prior elected body. It was unheard of to stop a project this far along. But these were unheard of times, and, after all, there was that horse-head thing.

That night, the president of the local community college (who was the managing partner of the project) and I stood at the podium for a public flogging for over an hour. It was horrendous and personally devastating. A politically organized group of a few local citizens, including a couple from my service club, filed one by one to the podium. Speaking under public comment, they made nasty remarks about the project or the chamber of commerce or the college or us personally. I found that something about being betrayed—especially in public—makes your face sting like a hard wind is blowing sand in your face.

I noted that the cast of characters were all part of the local democratic club and, yes, my local service club that previously supported the project and made a multiyear pledge for support. This was the same club that had supported my chamber chairman while his son was fighting in Baghdad; the same club where we had cooked hot dogs and hamburgers for the local fundraiser; and the same club that had sponsored the chamber leadership class.

Really?

But tonight, they portrayed us as liars and thieves. The public betrayal was bewildering. I kept thinking, *No one is winning here.* But I was wrong. There were plenty of winners—just not me, not our community, and certainly not the children who deserved better than plywood. This night would splinter the community and stall economic development for years to come. I felt very small.

Finally, the college president looked at me with pained eyes and said, "Linda, I've never seen anything like this. Have you had enough?"

I shook my head yes.

He approached the podium and, leaning down into the microphone, calmly beseeched, "We mercifully beg you to kill this project."

And in a 4/3 vote, they did.

In an instant, years and years of work were gone forever. The "suits" and I went outside and called a couple of the state legislators who had supported the project. We told them what had happened, and that tomorrow, we would begin unwinding the project and would try to give back the thirty million dollars.

Nobody could understand why. The Chairman of the county Democratic Club was in the audience and followed me out the door. Tugging at my arm, he asked why I had not called him.

"I could have stopped this," he said.

"I was too stupid to know it was about politics," I replied.

He looked at me and said, "Linda, everything is about politics."

Indeed, it is.

It would be years before we would understand what had happened and why. The next morning, I was up at dawn, watching the sunrise. We had cobbled together thirty million dollars to bring something to a community that had nothing—not even a place where more than 150 people could gather, and instead of being happy, they called us names and told us to send the money back. It was bewildering. The bean counters for the partners scratched their heads, not knowing how to account for sending money back. That doesn't usually happen.

When people realized what had happened, there was some push back from the community. Many of them desperately wanted this gathering place where our kids could graduate, and we could come together in large groups to watch our talented children perform. We were already well into the process of unwinding the project and giving back the money when the city manager of the city who voted to take back their money called. He said that maybe there was a chance to revisit the council decision and asked if I would I consider coming back to the table.

I graciously declined his offer. In a slightly intimidating voice, he suggested that it would be in my best interest to reconsider his offer. Aggravated, I quickly snapped that the public flogging we took at the city commission meeting had left a hole in my ass big enough to drive an eighteen-wheeler through, so if he thought another small bullet from him would bother me, he was sadly mistaken. He was quiet and then wished me a good evening before hanging up the phone. I wasn't about to go back into that mess.

I was mad but mostly haunted by the *why*. The *why* finally came for me in 2013. As the county struggled to plug a four-million-dollar deficit on the county-run convention center, I understood why our project had been killed. If it had been successful, the convention center would have had even more financial problems. So in essence, a good project had to be killed to save a bad one. It was slightly comforting to finally know that it wasn't about me. I was simply the champion of a project caught in the political crosshairs. The outcome was still the same; the betrayals, no less painful.

We returned the thirty million dollars, and I resigned from my service club. I couldn't stand to be in the same room with the people who had demonized me and still recited the pledge about the truth and friendships. And I also knew that even if I had disagreed with a project, I would have never publicly demonized a fellow service member. Once I had believed in that motto and in the people who had lunch together every week and recited the motto—not anymore.

I hardly believed in anything or anybody anymore. I was, by nature, trusting and idealistic. These new feelings were totally foreign to me. I was angry but scared as well. How would I navigate in a world that I no longer trusted? I wanted to talk about my anger. Instead, I quietly and graciously resigned. I doubt anyone ever noticed except the older gentleman who had recruited me. He asked to visit with me, and I told him the story—some of which he knew. He patted my hand, and, with tears in his eyes, he told me how sorry he was. He said that he was ashamed of an organization he had dedicated his life to. I told him that it didn't diminish anything that he had done or the good people that were still in the club. Most of them weren't even aware.

"But," he insisted, "it has, Linda. It has. Our organization isn't supposed to hurt people."

And then I realized that it was he who had instilled in me the value system of a community service organization. And he was the reason I took the high road and left quietly and graciously. I would have never disrespected him or all of the other good people. There was too much good work left to be done.

Back at the chamber office, I was trying to unwind the project while the media hounded me for comments. They wanted to start a media war between the chamber and the government partners.

I wasn't interested in fighting. I wanted to be left alone.

One day, a reporter called and asked me if I was outraged by the deliberate attack on the project. Sick of talking about the project, I replied, "And feel free to quote me on this. No. I'll tell you what outrages me: an innocent six-year-old girl who was kidnapped, molested, and buried alive in a garbage bag fifty miles from here this week—a little girl who died with her tiny fingers pushing holes through the bag. That is what outrages me, and that is what we all should be outraged at today—not a bunch of politicians who can't get along long enough to pull a community project together."

They never printed that quote. It was the last time they called me about the failed project.

Bottom Side Up

After I licked my wounds, I sorted people into two piles: those that I was mad at and those that I was not mad at. I placed the city manager from my city, the one that killed the project, in the "not-mad-at" pile. I called him and asked him to dinner. I wanted to apologize for that eighteen-wheeler comment. When I got to the restaurant, he was already drinking a scotch on the rocks. I assured him that I did not blame him for the project going south, and I was sorry for making the eighteen-wheeler comment. We laughed about it. He said that I was one tough lady.

I smiled. "Only when I'm pissed, and thankfully, that's not too often." We turned out to be good friends. It wasn't all that long before the elected officials turned on him. I sat with him the night he was fired. We laughed when he said he knew what the eighteen-wheeler felt like. Some years you're the dog, and some years you're the hydrant. I guess it was my year to be the hydrant.

I was pretty burned with politics, so I stayed as far away from them as I could, choosing to focus on my chamber members and the local economy. I was surrounded in the chamber office by such positive women. I felt an odd sense of relief at not having to worry about this project anymore. Now I would have to focus my attention on what to do about an aging chamber building that sat on city-owned land. I didn't trust politics enough now to spend much money on a building sitting on government-owned land. I had learned that the government has a lot more money for legal services than a nonprofit agency has. It's a battle you won't win.

Back at home, I had finally finished disposing of all of Mama's assets, including her house. Jerry was working at a low-paying computer job at a nonprofit. It seemed like something was wrong, but I thought it was just me. It seemed like I didn't know what the next right thing was.

2007

The Show Goes On, but It's not the Same

By mid-2007, I still had a feeling that something was not quite right. Life was going too fast, almost out of control. Despite the fact that I continued to lead an organization that was based on consumerism and economic development, internally, I wanted to slow down. The business community and the chamber members were becoming edgy. I could no longer control events. Everybody was doing their own thing—fast and furiously. At the time, I didn't understand why.

Still stinging from the Partnership Project fiasco, I internalized everything. I misinterpreted the community's collective anxiety for criticism of me. I wasn't as happy as I used to be. I did not understand at the time that we had entered into the "cycle of chaos."

One day, someone had scheduled a committee meeting to organize yet another event. Shortly before the meeting was to start, a weird hostage crisis arose in a supermarket a mile and a half from us. When the committee chair arrived and saw that no one else was there, she immediately began to tell me how it was my fault that nobody had showed up and questioned if had sent out notices. Aggravated, I snipped at her, "A mile and a half down the road, fourteen people are sitting in a circle in a locked-down supermarket, being held hostage by someone with a cell phone on a continent halfway around the world. The road is closed. For God's sake, this isn't about you or me!"

Stunned, she apologized, and we had coffee. She quietly shared with me that her company was going through a rough time, and she was being mandated to work more community events.

She was afraid that she might lose her job, and they had just bought a new house. It was a theme I would begin to hear as early as 2007. It made me uneasy.

At home, Jerry and I were working on a plan to pay off all our debt, including our home mortgage.

Real estate values were at an all-time high. I begged Jerry to sell everything and move back home to Tennessee while we could still get out. Much to my dismay, he wasn't about to budge. Our grandson had been born in 2001, and he stayed with us every weekend. Jerry had become very attached to him. After all, I was always working.

My chamber members seemed increasingly nervous, and in the next few months I would come to understand why. They lashed out a lot, demanded more, and sponsored less. My board members, "the suits," seemed tired and detached. I blamed it on the stress from the failed project and the strained relationship with local government.

But economically, things were changing locally and globally. Of course, I knew when the American employees started losing their jobs to foreigners that the global economy would change America.

One day, while on a fly-in to Washington to meet with congressional leaders, I was sitting at lunch with a federal department of transportation staffer. He asked me what I saw as the biggest issues in transportation. Clearly, he did not anticipate my answer.

"Just this very morning on the front page of our local newspaper was an article about us getting rickshaws in a beachside city. The Chinese are getting cars; we're getting rickshaws. I see that as a huge problem, sir."

"I see," he replied. "By the way, how is your lunch? Could you pass the raspberry vinaigrette, please?"

I graciously obliged. The rest of the lunch was cocktail talk.

The governments, both local and state, seemed in chaos as well. Florida had not yet recovered from the devastating hurricanes of 2004. Local governments were still fighting with FEMA for reimbursements for damage cleanup. Elected officials were generally in a bad mood. The floods had uncovered a host of vulnerabilities, including the local stormwater system and infrastructure, which had not kept up with the massive growth of the previous years.

The environmentalists had been right that we had grown too fast. Although, being a chamber of commerce chief, we were mostly opposed to each other's policies. Florida tax structure is based on growth and development. To slow down development would cause a construction-dependent economy to constrict, probably triggering a crisis. We would later watch that come to pass.

I had watched the technology bubble burst when Jerry lost had lost his high-tech job. It had been fast and hard. I now feared that the housing-market bubble would also burst. Florida did not have much diversity in its economical portfolio except tourism and construction. I watched and worried. The mortgage industry was pushing unsuspecting people to leverage the equity in their homes to buy other things: boats, new kitchen remodels, and expensive vacations. Jerry and I were paying off debt and saving cash.

Life is like a big ship.
Once it gets off course, it takes a long time to get it turned around.

Mama's death, the failed Partnership Project, the increasing demands of the chamber members, and the subtle downward spiral of the economy had left me exhausted. On the outside, I was still smiling, but on the inside, I was feeling empty and haunted. Fiercely protective of my community, I was scared for us, and I didn't know why.

I wrote "human-interest-story" letters in almost every chamber newsletter publication. One of the local papers always published my letters, which I titled, "Reflections." They were personal, authentic, and sometimes controversial. I wrote them anyway. In June of 2007, a man walked into the chamber office. He was, to me the "harbinger" of things to come.

I wrote the following article in the Chamber newsletter in July of 2007. The story was picked up by several news sources, creating a stir at the chamber and in the community.

Reflections of a Bible Verse and a Lotto Ticket

The day was warm and beautiful, an ordinary Florida day in June of 2007.

The chamber is always a revolving door of people, over 6,000 a year. They come with questions and dreams of starting a new business, seeking proof that they have moved to a good place, and most often, everyone is in search of a friendly face.

Our Chamber is the place that believes in people, in ideas, in the community, in the entrepreneurial spirit.

That day was no different, except for the gentleman who walked in the door to talk about his business.

The door was opened that day by the "harbinger."

That was the day I knew our world had quietly turned Bottom Side Up. We just didn't know it yet, or perhaps we did.

Most of the time, the chamber staff handles the walk-ins. We have a great business counseling program, and usually, we take the name and contact information and set up an appointment with one of our business counselors.

But that day, the gentleman's voice was like a siren, drawing me out of my office. I found myself walking toward him. I introduced myself and extended my hand to greet him. He looked tired and stressed but seemed relieved to shake my hand. He was polite and soft-spoken, midforties, clutching a small 3 x 5 photo album in his hand.

I smiled reassuringly, "So tell me what you do."

His face took on a strained expression, but his story rolled from his tongue as if he had found a safe place to talk. He shared that he had lost his job in Ohio. The economy was so bad there, he and his wife had decided to move to Florida about two years earlier.

He had researched all the demographics and decided to open a gift shop in the tourist district. But rent was expensive due to high property taxes and insurance, which he assumed was due to the 2004 hurricanes. He couldn't get the business to turn a profit, so he decided to close the business and start a residential painting and pressure-washing company. With such a good residential area, he was sure he could make a living, and his wife was going to nursing school. He had done everything right.

His eyes were sad when he told me that this business wasn't making it either. There was a quiet desperation in his voice, and he nervously caressed the small photo album as he spoke. "We're three months behind on the house payment. I expect the bank will take it soon. I don't know what we'll do when we lose the house. His eyes shifted downward to the floor as if he was too ashamed to look at me.

He was mostly sorry for his wife. He thought he had let her down. "I do good work, and I'm honest. I have "before and after pictures" here of some of the jobs I've completed, if you'd care to see them."

Without hesitation, I extended my hand to receive his photo album. He seemed pleased that I was interested. It was the least I could do for this stranger who had shared his pain so openly. As I opened his album, my eyes caught two items: a handwritten Bible verse and a lotto ticket. Seeing those two items pierced the veil of my understanding.

Bottom Side Up

I looked through his album. He was right. His work was good. I asked him if I could make an appointment for him with our business counselor. In my heart, I knew it wouldn't help. The sand had already run out of his hourglass. I guess he knew it too.

He graciously thanked me for my time and attention and said he would think about it. He quietly opened the door and walked away. I watched him until he disappeared, trying to process what I had just seen and felt. We never saw him again. I didn't expect to.

As I turned to walk back to my office, Georgette asked if he made an appointment. "No, I think he knows it's already too late."

Georgette, who is the wise and perceptive North Carolina girl with a gentle southern drawl, queried me, "Somthin' wrong?"

"He did everything right. He does good work; he promotes his product, and he can't find work. I think something very bad is happening to us."

"What makes you say that?" she pressed.

"I don't know. It's just a feeling." I made a strong pot of coffee. I do that when I need to ponder. His visit had left me haunted. It was no longer an ordinary day.

Back at my desk, strong cup of coffee in hand, and full of questions, I called a real estate agent and asked her if she was seeing anything different in the real-estate market. She said that real-estate prices, which had gone extremely high, had seemed to be coming down slightly and staying on the market a little longer. She didn't know if it was a trend or just a little dip.

I asked about foreclosures. Yes, they were seeing a few more.

"If we are indeed heading into a storm, we should bring our economic leadership together for a summit. It seems to me that the outer bands of the storm are already upon us."

The gentleman in my office is a nice man. He deserves more than a Bible verse and a lotto ticket. I hope one of them works because by myself, I have nothing else to offer him.

As always, Linda

The phone started ringing within hours of the article going public. My inbox filled up with comments and stories. Most of the nasty comments were from realtors and elected officials, angry that I would write such a negative article. But most were stories from people telling me how they had lost their jobs and their home. They had suffered in silence and shame. They were grateful that someone was finally seeing what was happening. I made a conscious decision that I would be their voice for as long as I could.

The public officials urged me to be more optimistic. I knew the bubble had already burst. I just didn't know how bad it would become. I wondered if they had any idea how this would affect their own government budgets. I was convinced that this was just the tip of the iceberg. They continued to talk about how great everything was, spending public dollars like drunken sailors.

It seemed to me that they must be talking through their ass because their heads were most assuredly buried in the warm Florida sand.

I continued to write and speak about the economy. I continued to call for an economic summit that never happened. I posed questions about the impact of the foreclosures on the community, the tax base, the education system, and quality-of-life issues. We tracked and posted foreclosure statistics as well as building permits in the chamber newsletter, much to the displeasure of some.

I asked people to share their stories. Realtors started to come to the chamber office to share quietly what they could not share publicly. Bravely, they gave voice to stories of events occurring inside houses that were void of people. It looked as though some had prepared and eaten a last meal, packed a few belongings, and vanished into the night, leaving behind family pets, dishes on the table, and pots of uneaten food on the stove. Some houses were completely empty with interiors destroyed, bleach poured on the carpets, light fixtures pulled from the ceiling, and cabinets pulled from the walls. The empty houses told the stories of those who had once lived there, piercing the veil of anger simmering in the souls of those who had lost jobs, and in those for whom disenchantment and anger was fueled by banks that were foreclosing.

The once-thriving sun belt had turned *Bottom Side Up*. There seemed now no good way out. A silent disaster was unfolding behind closed doors. Families all over America—and especially here in our community (just like the stranger in the chamber)—were "praying and buying lotto tickets" as they watched the sand run out of their hourglasses.

We were in the epicenter of a real-estate meltdown, and I had discovered the "canary in the coal mine." The ground was shaking underneath us, but I seemed like the only one who could see it or who was willing to talk about it. It was a lonely place to be. I felt helpless. It was like sitting idly by while watching the last grains of sand run out of an hourglass on a community that I loved.

This time, I didn't think anyone would turn the hourglass over.

Out in the community, there was a new phenomenon popping up called "networkers."—not the technical kind, the social kind. In hindsight, they were just searching for a place to belong.

They aggravated me because they took up so much energy. I later came to believe that they served a critical purpose. They at least gave us a false sense of security that we were not dying. Sometimes I referred to them as being "like a herd of grasshoppers."

They would gather up in a wad, move around the community to various businesses or restaurants like a band of gypsies—always eating and drinking and making merry. Business hosted them because in the old world, getting people into your business door translated to sales. In the *Bottom-Side-Up* world, it only translated to, "We hosted the networkers, and a good time was had by all." And then they would be off to the next place. However, had it not been for them, the silence would have been deafening. Looking back, I think they probably kept a lot of people from going crazy Chamber memberships were dropping. Renewals were off by 40 percent. Ad sales for the community directory were down by half. I watched the numbers and worried. But entrepreneurs are an active bunch. They always believe that hard work equals success. They called for more events and more action. My small staff tried to oblige, but we were exhausted. That Christmas, the business that was scheduled to host our large annual holiday affair called right after Thanksgiving. They reluctantly told me that their business was down so much they would not be able to host the Christmas event. It was scheduled for just two weeks later. They said they had been too ashamed to tell me about their business. They apologized for such short notice.

In my mind, I was thinking, *What in the hell am I going to do?* But beyond that, I felt so terrible for them because I knew that what was happening to them was happening to a lot of businesses. I told them I was sorry about business being so bad and wished them a "Merry Christmas." I said that there would always be next year. But by now, I didn't really believe it. I knew that by this time next year, there would be a lot of business people gone. It made me sad.

In another distant time, I would have called my elected friend and talked about the problem. Perhaps we could have done something more. But those days were over.

I called our ambassadors group together to tell them the Christmas event had been cancelled, and they told me that not having a Christmas event was unacceptable. So I took a few of our precious dwindling resources and threw a party. Bread and circuses—that's all they wanted. And so we threw a big party where we sang Christmas songs to karaoke. I was glad when the work festivities were finally over.

Bottom Side Up

Exhausted, I wanted to go home to Mama for Christmas. I wanted to cook with her and hand wash the dishes in the sink that looked over her backyard and tell her everything that I was feeling. But I couldn't go home for Christmas. Mama was gone. I was empty. I would have to sort it out on my own. Maybe, I tried to tell myself, I was wrong about it all.

2008

Hope is a Strategy.

On January 1, 2008, we all peeped through the door of the new year, anxious but still hopeful. The chamber board had decided to build a new chamber building rather than put any more money into repairing the old building we were in. Our plan was to sell the old building to the City (because they owned the land anyway) and finance the new building with small business incubator offices.

We already had a partnership with the Tourism Authority to run a welcome center, and we worked out a plan for the Small Business Assistance Center to rent space in our office as well. At the time, the plan seemed viable, even though the economy was steadily getting worse.

That plan would turn out to be the undoing of the Chamber.

The Chamber Alliance was preparing for Tallahassee Day, the annual event where we all went to schmooze the State Legislature—the same event where I had sat in the window when Mama was sick a few years back. My region of the county was the most dependent on the housing and construction market, so we had already been hit hard in the first wave of the meltdown. But as I mentioned earlier, we were a commuter community, and the real-estate industry as well as the elected officials

Bottom Side Up

wanted to keep it all under wraps. They thought it was just temporary. I was hoping that too.

Some of them demonized the failing businesses, saying they were probably not good business people anyway. The realtors just said of the increasing number of foreclosures that some people shouldn't be homeowners anyway. They sure didn't say that when they were selling them houses that were now *Bottom Side Up*.

As we were planning the menu for the Tallahassee reception, a wave of Mama's stubbornness washed over me. I closed my notebook and just simply announced, "I'm not going to Tallahassee this year."

Someone from the stunned group said, "Why Linda? You have to go to Tallahassee."

I matter of factly replied, "I don't, and I won't. Let them bring their honorable asses down here to my community and help me carry out boxes for the business people while they close their doors.

I'm not throwing a party while my people are going under."

And that was that.

I didn't go to Tallahassee, and they had the party without me, and no one noticed except a few who snidely remarked what a wonderful time they had. The show always goes on under the big top no matter what.

One by one, my Chamber members were closing their businesses. The economy was in a silent free fall, and I found myself in the absolute eye of the storm. I became a grief counselor to those losing their jobs, businesses, and homes. I comforted women after they buried their small-business-owning husbands and tried to help them sort through paperwork and decide what to do about the business. A few of them had died from stress or suicide. The times were silent and sad.

In a strange sidebar, I was picking out paint colors for the new Chamber building.

One morning, one of my long-time chamber members who owned a service company showed up at the Chamber unannounced. He was the kind of member that never asked for anything. He paid his dues, supported the community, and bought ads in the annual directory—a perfect member. He looked stressed and very tired. He wanted to talk to me. Dressed in his blue jeans, work boots, and logo-embroidered work shirt, he sat down and began. He had specialized in new service installations.

"Linda, you know I had a good business," he said, almost as if to convince himself. But in the past twelve months, he had seen work trickle down to nothing. Right after Christmas, he had laid off several of his employees. He said he had waited to get through Christmas because they had families and his employees had been like family to him. The man in the work boots took out his hand rag—the one he kept in his pocket to wipe grease while he worked—and dabbed at a tear that was about to roll down his cheek.

"I'm sorry," he apologized, "God, I don't want you to see me cry." He continued that he had a credit line attached to his home, and that the bank had adjusted the value of his home downward. Now he had nothing left in the credit line. He was *Bottom Side Up*.

"I'm probably going to lose my business and my house." He rolled the wadded hand rag back and forth as he talked. I asked him about changing his business to more repair than new installation. He said that his people weren't trained for repair, and he didn't have the money to train them.

It dawned on me that I was Vice Chairman of a technology center, and perhaps I could get a training program accelerated for repair technicians. I asked him to come back and see me the next week, and I would tell him if I had been able to get anything moving.

He looked at me and said, "I've always liked you. You've always been here for us. But I think it's too late." I hugged him, sweaty work shirt and all, and made him promise to come back. That was Tuesday.

On Wednesday night, he died in his sleep of a heart attack. I took his death hard. The picture of him wiping a tear with his grease rag haunted me. It still does. At his funeral, I felt sad and guilty.

I should have done something sooner. Had I eaten from the country club silver buffet lines too long? Had I forgotten my community? Did

I just not know how to use my power to make positive change? It was many, many moons before I came to understand that I was doing all that I could. I was fighting a battle that was invisible to most. I was pretty much alone.

I was pissed at the marketing messages suggesting that these businesses could get small-business loans. We were in the middle of an economic meltdown, and most of the people in charge didn't even know. I had to stop blaming myself.

As the year rolled on, more and more businesses closed. We had an e-mail chain of almost everybody who was closing a business. Anything that could be sold or given away was better than just walking away. Most of them said, "We've got some really good stuff." What they were really trying to say in their final moments was that they had been a legitimate business: "We were here, and we were real."

I tried to stop by on their closing days, just to pay my respects. I passed out hugs and words of encouragement. I asked them to call me if they needed to talk and gave them my cell phone number. I wanted them to know I cared about them as much on their closing days as I did the day they opened and paid chamber dues.

Mama always said that you know you had a love affair when you love someone more on the day they die than you did on the day you married. Based on those words of wisdom, I must have had a love affair with the business community.

As the businesses closed or tried to conserve cash, the Chamber cash flow was slowly declining as well. We were all beginning to worry about the mortgage payments that were going to be due early in 2009 for the new building. We had pretty healthy reserves, but they wouldn't last long if the trend continued. The "suits" suggested that we work harder to get the renewals in. They suggested that we start visiting the business members and encouraging them to get their dues in. I argued with them that I did not want to send my marketing director into some of these businesses, asking for money, not knowing what was going on.

It was only a few weeks after that conversation that one of our members who had not paid his dues murdered his stepson inside the business he owned, killed his wife, shot a police officer, and then killed himself. These were not ordinary times. But somehow, the women at the Chamber seemed to be the only ones that really understood the enormity of what was happening to the community.

In early November, as our business community hunkered down and the global economy teetered on the brink of collapse, my "frenemies" in local government (most of whom had been put into office by the democratic machine and the environmental community) smelled my vulnerability. They hated Chambers of Commerce—and especially a warrior for the business community like me. At the time, I was a registered Democrat, but I voted across all parties. I was not active in any formal partisan organization. Our local elections were not even partisan elections. I viewed myself more as a bridge across partisan lines, trying to build a consensus for community projects.

But in the game of politics (and that now seemed to be the only game), no opportunity is ever lost, and no good deed goes unpunished.

I knew a few remarkable political leaders that did not dish out retribution, but they seemed to be getting fewer and fewer. They quickly organized another public flogging of me and began to pull our public funding. When the clandestine decision was made to cancel the contract for our visitors' center, we found out the night before. Like a lamb going to slaughter, I walked in to the meeting thinking that I would (or could) defend my position. We had just moved into the new building, based on their partnership. I certainly did not want to lose the funding. Instead, the public flogging began.

One of the Authority advisory members suggested in a public meeting that I was never anywhere. Little did she know or care that the prior week I had been in a garage with a widow whose husband had committed suicide, and I was trying to help her sort through his business papers. Her comment rolled through my blood like a heat wave. I started to rise to comment, but another of my Chamber Chief friends, sitting next to me—she was also losing her funding—leaned over and gently whispered, "Please don't get up. You'll slide right up her ass."

One thing for sure, I have been cursed with a few enemies, but I have also been blessed by a whole bunch of wise friends. I took her advice and stayed seated. And just like that, the money was gone. The Visitors' Center would be closed in January, just as we were getting settled into the new building. They thought I would continue serving the visitors without funding, but they were mistaken. I called the three cities in my political region and informed them of our plight. I asked them to assist with keeping the Visitors' Center open. I told them I didn't think the small-business community should have to support the tourism industry when they were the ones collecting bed tax. It was like taxing the business community twice, and I wasn't going to do it.

Nobody cared. I was fighting regulations on behalf of the business community, so the governments were hoping we would go under anyway.

During the Christmas holidays, with the world holding its breath, hoping the entire economy wouldn't melt down, we held a festive Grand Opening for the new Chamber building. I asked a local pastor to offer prayers for our community at the ribbon-cutting ceremony. It was to be my first and last Christmas in the new Chamber building. Looking back, I think I knew that all along.

2009

*I mean, maybe under the surface,
somewhere that's hard to see,
I've known that it had to end for a long time. I just never
thought I'd be the one to end it.*

—SUSAN COLASANTI, WAITING FOR YOU

A small business development center had agreed to rent space in our building to assist the business community with business education classes. They were supposed to be bringing in business resources, helping businesses apply for loans, reorganize their business, etc.

In early January, I met with the business development director and looked over his programming schedule. We were still working on the "Memorandum of Understanding" that we had started over six months before that. He would teach classes and charge a fee, and we would split the proceeds. Knowing that our community had been wounded in the meltdown, I told him that his programming was outdated and needed to be retooled for a post-meltdown business community.

"I'm not going to bring them in to talk to a bunch of bankers that have no intention of giving them a loan. It's just an exercise in futility, and they don't have the energy." The banks had just pulled in their credit lines, especially the ones that had been secured by a second mortgage. I continued, "Why would we give the business owners false hope? We need to be helping them decide how to crash-land their planes and save what little they have left."

I knew it was just a shell game for class numbers. The outcomes didn't matter to anyone except me. And what I thought didn't seem to matter anymore either. I noticed the director looked at me like I had two heads. After that meeting, the dialog with them suddenly stopped.

Their money was in my budget, and it wasn't coming in, leaving another bleeding hole in the bottom line. I called and asked for a meeting.

Looking across the table at him, I simply said. "Tell me the truth, you're not coming, are you?"

He shook his head no.

I said, "It's about your numbers, isn't it? My community is down, and they can't give you the numbers you need, so you're not coming." The question—very loudly—went unanswered.

His boss later told me that it was because I had changed the configuration of the office space.

I admitted that I did. I put the business counseling space right next door to the conference room for his convenience.

I just glared at him. "You get hundreds of thousands of dollars of state and federal money to help the business community, and you turned your back on my wounded business community because I moved the counseling office next to the conference room? That's just bullshit. And by the way, your program needs to be retooled. It's not relevant during an economic meltdown. I'm not going to promote a program to my business community that costs money and doesn't work."

He gave the standard training answer: "I'm sorry you feel that way. Let me know if there's anything else we can do for you."

I told him that I doubted there would be because the Chamber was going down with the business community. My happy disposition had been gone for several months. I wasn't in the mood for cocktail talk or bullshit. I hated it, but lately, I seemed to cuss more than I smiled.

The Visitors' Center was gone; the Small Business Development Center was gone. I tried to find other partners to move into the Chamber office. I could see the sand running out of the hourglass.

If I had still been in the good graces of my political friends, this wouldn't have been happening. It wasn't as much economics as it was politics.

I reviewed the real-time statistics faithfully: the building permits, the real estate monthly report which included number of houses sold, and the price, days on the market, and the foreclosure report from Realty Trac. They pulled the curtain back on everything. The stats made me queasy, but I couldn't stop watching. The government (HAL) was still responding to lag data eighteen months behind.

Note to self: Lag data ain't worth a damn in a crisis, and don't let anybody tell you it is—even if that person has a PhD behind his or her name.

Searching for the truth about what was really happening to us, I took my questions directly to the people. I knew full well (Mama taught me that term) that the government would only respond to politics and lag data, and that was the useless kind of information that we, the community, were going to get. It's an awful way to make decisions. I knew the only way to know the real truth was through that messy stuff—anecdotal data—the stuff of which life and chambers are made. It's real and raw and full of emotion, but dammit, if you want to know what's really going on, ask the local chamber of commerce or somebody whose "ox is being gored."

Mama said the truth always comes out when your ox is being gored. I never really understood what that meant, but, generally, I guessed it was when something really bad was happening to you. People trusted me because they knew they could. They told me everything. They knew

I would keep their confidence. That's why this book has been hard to write. I want to tell their story without violating their confidence.

"Elvis Is Dead, and I Ain't Feeling Too Good Myself"

It was early February when I got my usual upper respiratory infection. I was too busy to nurse a cold. Besides, my doctor had died suddenly in December, and I wasn't crazy about going through the process of finding another doctor. I was too busy and I was pissed and sad that my doctor (whom I adored) had died.

Antihistamines make my heart do funny stuff, and a new doctor always gets too excited, thinking I'm having a heart attack. My old doctor understood me. But he was gone, and I was just hoping my cold would go away. January had been the usual whirlwind of events. It was the mother of all months at the chamber. Usually, I worked the entire month without a day off.

There was the annual chamber meeting and the board installation, followed by the MLK celebrations, followed by the annual manatee festival. Additionally, the year-end books had to be closed, followed by getting prepared for the annual audit.

Money was very tight, and the board was not in a good mood. I wasn't either. My mind had turned to survival mode and had run a thousand miles a minute, searching for solutions. The community was chaotic. My phone rang constantly, and my inbox overflowed with e-mails. The community was nervous and reaching out to anyone who still had a live person answering the phone. I was emotionally exhausted and still sick. I couldn't shake that virus thing.

I woke up one night to go to the bathroom, and when I started back to bed, I was so dizzy that I had to hold on to the wall. I knew something was very wrong. I was too sick to even go to the doctor. I stayed in bed for three days, flat of my back, hoping the dizziness would subside. My ear ached, and I had a fever. Finally, I was able to get to a doctor—one that had moved into my real doctor's office and had taken over his patients.

He told me I had a virus, perhaps the swine flu, an inner ear infection, and an ear drum that had burst.

"How long do you think it will take this dizziness to go away?" I asked.

"This is severe, Mrs. White. You may be looking at three to six months. You are going to need lots of rest."

"You gotta be kidding me," I snapped.

And all the while I was thinking, *Well that's a fine damn predicament to be in when you're trying to save a community organization of six hundred members, the jobs of five women, and your personal career.*

We were scheduled to go before the City Council on Tuesday night to formally request their purchase of the old Chamber building. We already had a plan in place and had an appraisal done on the building. It was a complex situation. The City contributed nothing to the Chamber, but more importantly, neither I nor any of my Board of Directors had supported the campaign of the newly elected mayor, who was, by the way, a democrat and wasn't fond of chambers of commerce anyway.

I had never thought much about partisan politics at the local level until the past few years, and I certainly had never seen the Chamber as a partisan organization. It was an awakening for me. Lord knows, I should have seen it coming. This was merely another opportunity for a public flogging and to have all of us grovel to someone we had not politically supported. I generally was the one at the podium. Politics had gotten so bad that I didn't really want my board members to have their names and the names of their business drug through the mud in the media. I had one of the finest Boards of Directors in the county. I was pretty protective of them, which, by the way, was my job.

So here I was, dizzy as a drunken sailor and *Bottom Side Up*. This was going to be a critical meeting. We needed to get the building issues resolved in order to put some money into our coffers.

It was Thursday. Surely I would be better by the following Tuesday. The untimely illness had only added to my stress. I slept most of the weekend. Between naps, I was negotiating a deal with God: "If I rest this weekend, will you let me be better by Tuesday?"

Bottom Side Up

I'm guessing that answer was 'no.' Just like the new doctor predicted, I was not better by Tuesday. I had been working from home on my laptop, propped up by pillows. The dizziness was not so bad if I didn't try to walk—duh. Stubborn woman that I am, on Tuesday afternoon, I got off the sofa at home, put on my business suit and high heels, and went to the Chamber office.

I was going to march right into that city council meeting, walk right up to that podium, take my public flogging, make our deal, and fall back into bed—*not!*

This was not the day to be weak of heart or soul. I made it to the office, but by the time I got there, I couldn't stand up. When the "suits" arrived, they found me lying on the floor, flat on my back, laid out all pretty in a business suit and heels, and with a little red airline pillow under my neck, truly *Bottom Side Up*.

The image of seeing the "suits" standing over me, asking me if I thought I could get up, will be branded in my mind forever. The sad thing was that I was ashamed I was letting them down. Trying so hard not to let them know how sick I was, I addressed the problem with my usual sharp wit and told them this was the new leadership position. We all laughed. But in my mind I was thinking: *This is not funny.* I advised them that they would have to go before the city council by themselves. They were quite capable. I just hated to see them demonized.

I listened, flat on my back in suit and heels, as they stood over me and strategized about who would make the presentation to the city council. Bad political relationships are like a bad marriage—only everything is public. I was mad about being sick at such an inconvenient time. I thought Fate was conspiring against me. In retrospect, I was exhausted: burned out—body, mind, and soul. I had watched the economic meltdown of my entire community and had been beaten down in the public from elected officials who were so consumed by their own arrogance and power. The grief had consumed me.

I somehow managed to drive myself home, and the "suits" made the presentation. They got the deal done, but the City kept dragging its feet about cutting the check. It would be remitted to us in installments. We would have to beg every time, I was pretty sure. Foot dragging, by the way, is a very common political strategy. As the bureaucrats say, "Let's just wait the bastards out." The bastards are generally the people.

The cash flow was down to a trickle. The Executive Board met and asked me to lay off some of my staff. I asked them to lay off their staff. Bewildered they looked at me and said, "Linda, you are our staff."

"Exactly," was my reply. "I can't save a failing organization without a staff. I can't possibly run events, answer the phone, do the bookkeeping, and be the community face." I explained again about the bookkeeping. Bookkeeping is labor intensive in a chamber of commerce because it has thousands of small entries. One "Eggs and Issues" breakfast meeting could create seventy-five bookkeeping entries— not to mention ad sales and sponsorships and special events. Chamber bookkeeping is a nightmare. It's not about money; it's about quantity.

"I'm not worth a dime to you if I don't have my staff. So fire me and keep them." Looking back, I now know that I was just trying to avoid the pain and shame of the actual closing. But my plan failed. They would not let me go. So I did the unthinkable. I asked for my pay to be cut in half. Most of my staff had children. At least it was only Jerry and me. Sandy was a widow and was raising her grandchild. I had to buy us all a little time. I met with community leaders, the hospital, elected officials— everyone that should have mattered. None of them really believed me when I told them we were not going to make it without a cash infusion from the community. We tended not to be able to grasp what was happening around us until it was too late to make a difference.

Mama always said, "You never miss the water until the well runs dry."

The Mayor and I were on friendly terms, despite the political payback he inflicted upon me. He brought me chocolate one day because he knew I wasn't feeling well. I graciously accepted the chocolate, but I wanted the damn check. But then he knew that, right? We talked about the state of the community and my illness, and then I broached the subject of the payment for the building.

"Well, we'll get around to that," he said.

I said "Mayor, I've already cut my salary in half to try to keep this place open and functioning. We will have to shut these doors if we don't get some help. The business community is wounded. Our community is wounded. I'm not in the mood for political games. Surely, you do not want your Chamber of Commerce to close."

"You love this place," he responded. "You aren't going to shut it down."

Obviously, he did not understand the impact of the meltdown on the business community. After all, they were still paying taxes to the government (HAL). And obviously he did not understand that love and money are two completely different things.

Leaning over my desk and looking him straight in the eye, I replied, "Mayor, believe me, I *will* land this plane in your Hudson River." Then I opened the box of chocolate and offered him a piece. "Which kind of filling do you favor?" I smiled. Later that week, the first installment of the deal came. It was too little too late.

If you are driven by the approval of others, you will also die by their rejection.
—AUTHOR UNKNOWN

I wished a thousand times that I could get drunk. I get sick before I get drunk, and I made my mind up a long time ago not to put my face where my butt usually sits, so I watched the decimation of my community and my Chamber—sober and in real time. Our community had entered the cycle of chaos. The pace was frenzied and overwhelming. At nights, I would climb into bed and immediately fall into an exhausted sleep, only to wake forty-five minutes later, heart racing and my "to-do" list scrolling in my head like a bad movie.

Our grandson was still coming every weekend—mostly because he had become Jerry's whole life, and the Chamber and the community had become my whole life. I desperately needed some down time, and I was angry that I couldn't get it. An ADHD child with oppositional defiance and a community in crisis don't allow much time for rest and relaxation. It seemed like the world had inserted a tube into my chest, and it was sucking the very "life force" out of my body. Every damn body wanted me to do something or fix something. The phone was ringing by 7:00 a.m. every morning. I felt like I had lost my life to some unknown force.

I decided to see a mental health counselor and chose a woman who had a soft, gentle way. I hungered for gentleness and safety. I wanted to stay in her office—forever.

I didn't realize I was so exhausted and wounded. Since Mama had gone, I had no safe place to talk about my life. All of my feelings were pent up. There was no place to process. I spilled over onto the kind counselor like a pitcher that couldn't stop pouring. She told me that she understood my exhaustion and burnout. She shared that she felt it too. Her husband pastored a church that was failing, and everybody was screaming at them. She said that she wanted desperately to hide too.

Calmly, she told me the bad news was that she could not fix me. The good news was that I had the power to fix myself. Secretly, I wondered why she didn't fix her own self (a few weeks later, she did). I told her I was too tired and too sick to fix myself. I was still trying to hide the fact that I was sick and dizzy most of the time.

"Small steps," she said. "Small, gentle steps." My first assignment was just to make my bed every morning. For the past few years, I had not done that. Mornings were too chaotic, and I was always on the phone. I couldn't believe that I was paying seventy-five dollars an hour for a counselor to tell me to make my bed. Mama always made me make my bed every morning before school, and her bed was always made, even when she was sick.

Looking back, Mama's life had not seemed so chaotic. Maybe making your bed is the secret to life. I was willing to try anything. Seeking simplicity, I purchased a new white bedspread, a boring one—just like my grandmother had—and started making my bed every morning. Strangely, I had found something I could control. I felt a shift—a very tiny shift, but anything was good. For five minutes in an otherwise *Bottom-Side-Up* world, I was in control.

March came and went like a blur. I was still battling dizziness and exhaustion and cash flow. I had lost the hearing in my right ear. If the doctor was correct, I would be this way until August—maybe longer. I made my biweekly visits to the nice woman counselor. I told her that I felt angry and alone and overwhelmed, and that I was pretty certain we were going to lose the Chamber. She understood. Not only was she a counselor, but she was a woman living in the same place that I was. She said that we were normal people, in caregiving positions, living in very "abnormal times," watching people we cared about going through awful things.

In one of our sessions, I told her it was like being waterboarded every day. I was watching people lose it all while knowing "full well" that the same fate would one day come to me. It seemed as though we bonded (the counselor and I). It seemed that I had given voice to her feelings. After all, where does a counselor go to cry? In early April, she advised me that this would be our last session. She and her husband were leaving the area. They were going someplace else where the economy wasn't so bad. They would start over. I hugged her and said, "I'm glad you're getting out."

She told me that my anger was just part of my grief at watching our community and my own life die, and that she had felt it too. I started to cry and muttered the words that I am always too stubborn to say: "I'm scared."

Handing me a tissue, she said, "I know, and you have every right to feel that way. These are scary times for all of us."

So now my doctor was dead, and my counselor was moving. I went to my dentist of fourteen years and said, "You're not leaving too, are you?"

His reply was, "I hope not."

No one was sure of anything anymore.

For the month of April, our accounts receivable was down 65 percent. I had never seen anything like that before. Something very, very bad was happening to us.

I got up early one morning and went to the place I called the pulse of the community—the local convenience store. Early in the Florida mornings, construction workers, trying to beat the midday heat and the afternoon thunderstorms were out early, getting fueled up for the day with sodas and cigarettes and gas. The community commuters to Orlando stopped in for gas and coffee. That morning, I noted that the traffic was light—not like the congested lines that we had protested against for years. Pulling into the convenience store, I backed into a parking spot for my vantage point. I walked into the store to get my own coffee and to speak with the store clerk. I wanted to know what she was seeing, and if she could confirm what I thought. The store traffic was light. She spoke freely to me about how the construction industry had trickled down to nothing.

"They don't come anymore," she said. Then she shared her own story of having worked in this store almost eight years. Her son-in-law, who had worked in construction, had been laid off, and her daughter, who had worked in Orlando, had recently lost her job as well. Her husband was diabetic, and they had no health insurance. She poured out to me that she had an abscessed tooth and was hoping to be able to go to the dentist when she got paid. She figured that it would take most of her paycheck. Her daughter, son-in-law, and grandchild had just moved in with them.

"Times are bad," she said. "You, working for the Chamber of Commerce and all, do you think you can help? You're the only person I've seen that was 'somebody' who acted like they even knew what was happening to all of us."

I reached over and touched her hand. "We just all have to try to do the best we can." I thanked her for sharing her story, told her that her family was lucky to have her, and that I hoped her tooth got better. Back in the car, sipping my coffee, watching the comings and goings in and out of the convenience store—or the lack thereof—I wanted to go back into the store and give the clerk the money to go to the dentist. But after this morning, I was pretty sure that I would not have a job or dental insurance very long myself.

Back in the office, I called our CPA to come to the office to meet with me. I asked him to look at the drop in the accounts receivables. He asked if I was sure we had sent out billing. I confirmed that we had. He said that he had not seen anything like it either. I told him I thought we were at "Ground Zero" in the economic meltdown, and the business community was hunkered down, conserving any cash they could.

We sent out a letter to the members, asking them to remit their dues if they could. Nothing happened. The CPA met with the board to confirm the critical nature of our situation. We shifted into crisis-response mode, making every decision together. I e-mailed them the accounts receivable every day. It was waterboarding for them too. At the instruction of the executive board, we were already paying everything we could by credit card, which later turned out to be a monumental issue for me.

At the end of June 2009, the cash flow was down to a trickle. I could see the end from here. The accounts receivables had dropped by 85 percent. Our bank had closed our line of credit, although we had put $150,000.00 down on the building only six months earlier. The Florida housing market had officially crashed, and our bank was going into receivership as well. We worked furiously to try to sell the building to some investors who could make the payments and we could rent the space from them until the economy picked up. But because the bank went into receivership, everything was frozen.

Like an unexpected rose blossom frozen by a late winter ice storm, there was nothing left to embrace except the end. I took a trip to one of my favorite places—a cabin in Tennessee, overlooking a beautiful lake. I went there to mentally prepare for the end. This was a game-changing decision I had to make. I wanted to be sure I got it right, and that I could know that I had done the right thing. The ending would be brutal and very public. It was the same as all the other significant endings I had experienced, and I wanted to do it with as much grace as I could muster.

Mama always told me that it's hard to muster up grace. As usual, she was right. I wanted to leave the women who worked for me whole. I did not want them to feel guilty or wounded, even though I knew all too well that they would grieve. They loved their jobs, and they loved being at the center of the community. The closing would be a public event, which would make it harder.

The cabin was comforting. Away from the streetlights, I could count the stars. I could see the Milky Way and the Little Dipper. I wished that I could see God, but I just felt alone. I didn't even think He was looking. I called my stepdaughter and asked her to bring the grandchildren to the cabin. We made s'mores, and they kissed me with wet popsicle kisses. Children and puppies—they don't care if you're successful or not. They love you anyway. And that unconditional love was what I needed. Messy smiling faces and dirty sticky hands—they'll heal you every time, if you let them.

After they went home, I worked on the final exit strategy. I prayed for grace, but I didn't think God was really listening. I guess that's why Mama said we "muster our own grace." That's when you do the right thing—even when nobody's looking. I remembered back to when my paternal grandfather (Papa) had died. Papa had lived with us my whole life.

That's how we roll. No nursing homes for us—we take care of our own.

It was November, and the community had been hit by a brutal cold spell and a flu epidemic. It was a ritual in our farming community for the men of the community to dig the graves of those who had passed. But that week, all of our neighbors were sick. I found Daddy in Papa's bedroom, crying. I asked him what was wrong, and he said that he had to go dig Papa's grave. He wept as he told me, "Nobody should have to dig their own daddy's grave."

That memory must have been triggered by the similarity of my own situation—the enormity of preparing a grave for something you love and feeling so totally alone. There was a lump in my throat as I finished writing the exit strategy. The task at hand did not get easier. On Saturday, we packed our bags and travelled back to Florida. I was grateful for the fourteen-hour drive. We made most of it in silence. Jerry was not a big talker anyway—especially about things that were *Bottom Side Up*.

Bottom Side Up

On Monday, Jerry and I returned to our respective jobs. I called my regular Monday morning staff meeting. I knew this would be the last one. The morning found me whispering another prayer. This one was for grace—grace to say the right words to my staff, to not cry, to think clearly, to speak confidently, and to empower them with strength and courage to face their new unknown futures. They, like me, would need to construct new baskets to hold whatever was left of themselves. I would tell them the truth and let them react however they needed to. I would not take it personally. Then I would ask the chairman of the "suits" (i.e., board) to convene an emergency meeting that evening, and I would present a couple of options to them—neither of which would be good.

After the tearful staff meeting, I returned to my office. It was 10:00 a.m. My cell phone rang, and it was Jerry. He quickly reported that he had just lost his job. I responded with an unbelievable question: "Are you shitting me?"

To which he responded with a very sarcastic but honest question, "Would I shit you about losing my job?" And there we were, in an instant, once again *Bottom Side Up*.

The scenario was too unbelievable to even process. I made a strong pot of coffee and tried to comfort my staff. I couldn't even think about myself. I would do that another day. I wrote the agenda for the evening emergency meeting and made copies for the "suits."

My birthday would be in four days. I know I've said it before, but it seems like all the bad things always happen to me in July. I was numb and fiercely focused on getting the task in front of me finished. That task was ending my life as I knew it as the chamber of commerce CEO. It seemed a bit cruel to me. It would have been easier if the "suits" had just fired me. But in some kind of cruel twist of fate, I was assigned the task of the corporate euthanasia. It was like being asked to load the gun for your killer. I obliged them.

Linda S. White

Perhaps I Had Known All Along

Earlier that year, I had asked the chairman of the "suits," who was a long-time trusted friend, to resign his position. When he asked me why, I told him there was no way the chamber would make it. I reviewed the financials and my projections. I told him that I thought the economy was very bad nationally—but especially locally. Being a community banker, he agreed. He knew the state of the economy all too well. He was struggling to keep his own bank alive.

Little did we know that just a couple of years later, he would be testifying before congress on behalf of community banks all over America. He would try to give voice to their struggles and explain why they were so important to communities.

Without emotion, I told him, "Bad things will have to be done to me. You will never forgive yourself. I would rather the bad deeds be done to me by someone other than my friend. I don't want to wind up hating you."

We both came from farming families. He understood how to have a serious conversation with few words and little emotion. He obliged and submitted the letter of resignation letter that I had already written for him. Quietly and unceremoniously, the vice chairman, who was a fairly new board member, took his place. He was not so attached to me or the community. The tough decisions would be easier for him and for me.

I stand before you a tower of strength, the weight of the world on my shoulders.
As you pass through my life, look, but not too close, for fear I will expose the vulnerable me.
—DEIDRA SARAULT

As planned, the "suits" assembled that evening in a very somber mood. It was five o'clock in the afternoon. I could hear Mama in my head: "Try to hold up."

Like a steel magnolia, I tried to make it easy on the "suits." It kept my mind off my own pain. They barely looked at me. Many of them were not only "suits," they were also my best friends. As horrible as it was for me, I knew they hated it just as badly. It was like having to put the family dog to sleep. I was sure this would be a haunting memory, and it has been—at least for me. I have never discussed it with any of them.

That fateful evening in July, the Chairman called the last meeting to order. I stood before them without emotion, reading bullet point by bullet point the sequence of events of the closing. I should have felt sorry for me; instead, I felt sorry for them. They didn't sign up to turn out the lights. The meeting was brief. I stood without emotion before them as they followed the procedure I had prepared. I gave them two options: terminate all the staff, liquidate the assets, pay the bills, transfer the membership, and close the Chamber; or terminate all the staff, close the doors for a few weeks, bring in someone to reorganize the organization, negotiate with the bank, try to start over, and wait for the political leadership to turn over and perhaps get a few "friendlies' in office.

At any rate, I wanted my name off of everything, which meant that someone else would have to accept the responsibility. They asked if I thought there was any other way. In my early life in health care, there were only two circumstances that allowed someone to stop CPR once it was started: either the one giving CPR was too exhausted to go on or a person with decision-making authority deemed that there was no need to go on. Answering their question with confidence, I said, "The community is too wounded to help us. Nobody is coming. It's not that they won't; it's that they can't. I don't see any other options other than the ones I have provided to you."

I didn't look up. The motion was made and seconded to close the Chamber and terminate the staff.

Motion approved.

And with that it was over. It was only in retrospect that I realized how exhausted they all were from trying to save their own businesses. They filed out quietly and in a somber manner. I was left to dig the grave.

I had given my staff of wonderful women the choice of participating in the "putting down" of the beloved organization or escaping the pain of the final acts by simply taking a pink slip. They all chose to stay. On the final day, one chose to leave; the other three, fiercely, efficiently, and sadly assisted me as we made the final preparations. I hugged each one of them many times during the day, telling them how awesome and strong and talented they were. I repeated to them over and over, "This was not your fault."

No one from the Board, not one single "suit," showed up on the final day. No meetings with BHGs ("Big Hairy Goals"), as they liked to call them. No more visioning sessions, No strategic planning, No final curtain call. No plaques or certificates of appreciation. No going-away party.

I was full of emptiness. Indeed, we all are mostly alone when the sand runs out of the hourglass.

Ten years of accommodating elected officials, board members, and the community at large—but that day, the phone was quiet, except for the media (wanting the story) and another organization, wanting my database. Only the vultures lingered to pick any remains that might be useful. Inside, the four of us left standing were making the final preparations. We ordered in our last meal of pizza. I picked up the tab. What do you do on your last day?

It was hard to comprehend that after this day, we would be erased. There would be no remaining personnel file, no place for a new employer to call to hear about my good works, and no place to verify my years of employment—nothing. It was not something I understood.

That was the day I really understood about death and funerals and why we put up monuments and carve our names on trees—and even why we write our names on bathroom walls. Because none of us can comprehend what it is like not to have ever existed. But all that was emotional, and I had to focus on the tasks at hand: submit payroll, electronically transfer the database of members to another chamber so that the members wouldn't lose their money, electronically transfer financials to the CPA, e-mail the inventory list to the "head suit in charge," and make sure that the CPA has all the information for the w-2s. It was July, but in January there would be no chamber to issue tax information.

That was good thinking on my part. The following January, the Chamber would not even exist, and the "suits" would have gone on to leading something else. The "suits" could not escape the final act. The CEO would be officially dead and erased. She could make the final arrangements, but she could not actually dispose of her own body. The "suits" could not delegate this final act of disposing of the assets and filing the paperwork.

The last day went by fast.

Our insurance agent (who was also my "explainer of all things Jewish" and had a great deal of insight into life) stopped by that morning to talk to me. He reminded me of the story of Moses, who drug the Israelites through the desert for years while they complained about everything. He said that he really believed that Moses was tired of the people and didn't really mind that he didn't get into the "Promised Land" with them because he was tired of them anyway. So God let him rest on the rock and watch them from afar, peeking over into the "Promised Land" every now and then.

Smiling, I said, "Are you comparing me to Moses?"

He laughed and said, "You catch on quick. You've drug this bunch around, trying to build this community for a long time, perhaps now you can rest."

I appreciated his words and his desire to say something comforting to me. And I felt better about Moses too.

Mama always told me to never schedule a funeral in the morning. She said people move slow, and the day goes by fast. As usual, Mama was right.

As we approached the final moments, I prepared the obituary and final words to the community. I gave one last phone interview to the local newspaper. And then, with a slow, deep breath, for the last time, I pressed *Send*.

Linda S. White

STATEMENT FROM THE CHAMBER

Dear Chamber Member and Community Leaders:

It is with much sadness that we inform you of the closing of the Chamber of Commerce, effective July 2, 2009.

As you all know, the local economy was fueled by the real-estate and construction markets, which began to struggle as early as 2007. When the new Chamber office was built, it was done so with an agreement from the Tourism Authority to house a Visitors' Center and the Small Business Development Center.

At the end of January, due to economic issues, the Tourism Authority cancelled a long-standing partnership, and the Small Business Development Center decided not to move into the Chamber building.

Within another 30 days, longstanding advertising support from the Economic Development Department and the County Airport was cancelled as well. The snowball effect continued with print media and major corporations pulling long-standing support early in 2009, citing economic concerns.

The Chamber of Commerce has served this community with integrity and has dedicated its resources to strengthening its business community and building local and regional partnerships that would help define the community as a region, both geographically and politically. It was our vision that this would bring much-needed resources to our area for infrastructure and quality of life amenities.

Our Board and Staff have worked fiercely to try to save the organization, making many cuts, which included the CEO cutting her own salary 50 percent to try to save the organization and staff positions. However, as we continued to try to assist others, we eventually succumbed to the same fate that hit so many of our members. The Chamber has always strived to be part of the collective community during the good times, and we have been part of the collective community, sharing and experiencing the pain of some very bad times.

Bottom Side Up

This closing, as with any event, will evoke many feelings within the community. Some of you will be sad; some of you will be mad; some of you will be glad; and for some of you, it will be a non-event. Any and all of those feelings are normal and expected responses.

In closing, on behalf of the Chamber Board and dedicated Chamber staff, we offer Prayers for our community, Good-byes for our Friends, and Best Wishes to all.

—Linda White, President, CEO

Together, my staff and I turned out the lights. They stood at my side as I locked the door for the last time. We hugged each other and walked toward our cars. It occurred to me that day that we were facing a setting sun. I had never thought about it before. The silence was loud. No good-bye speeches, no going away party, no certificates of appreciation, no severance package, and not even the ability to participate in COBRA insurance plan. When everything is gone, there is no COBRA plan.

No "suits" could be found—only us and loud silence.

Let your tears come. Let them water your soul
—EILEEN MAYHEW

The crepe myrtles were in full bloom. The one we dedicated to Georgette's mama when she died was especially beautiful that day. We waited while Georgette broke off a bloom and carried it in her hand to her car. There we stood, watching her like a bunch of "Steel Magnolias." The most beautiful women I had ever known—and even in the good-bye moment, I whispered to the universe, "Thank you for them." I would never again tell them, "See you tomorrow."

Watching them for the last time, the essence of their personalities ran through my mind. Sandy, a feisty lady from Boston who had survived being a young widow and raising two children and now two grandchildren, had an infectious laugh. She loved to cook and watch sports. She was the most hot tempered of the three and could sometimes get sharp with that Boston accent. When she got mad about something, she would always say, "the 'damn bastads.'" Georgette called her Miss McPhillipet on days when she was sassy. I would walk in the door, and Georgette would say, "Mornin' Miss White. Milk is same price today as a gallon of gas, damn near four dollars." And if Sandy was in a bad mood, "George" would add, "And Miss McPhlippet is in her office today." Sandy was smart and stubborn and somehow always managed to have a great purse and a clean car. After her husband died, she painted the outside of her house for a year. Sometimes it would be at least two colors. Somehow, it got her through the rough spots. Georgette and I always tried to get Sandy to put more *R*s in her words. Helen, a smart and stylish lady from New York, the one I had hired in my early days at the city, would just say, "Why y'all give a damn about *R*s?"

Helen was smart and strong, and she loved solving problems for people. She also had a wicked sense of humor that I loved.

Georgette, tall and beautiful in the simplest kind of way, was from North Carolina. She, like Sandy and Helen, had a wild sense of humor. I called Georgette the chamber goddess.

Sandy called her mother, "Ma."

Helen called her mother, "My mother."

Georgette, a southern girl like me, called her mother, "Mama."

Like a funeral processional, we each, one by one, drove out of the parking lot onto the highway. I was the last in line behind them. My heart broke open as I watched them making their final exits and wiping back tears. I was barely able to get out of the parking lot before the hot tears began to roll down my own face. The past year had seemed like one long funeral, and finally, the bell had tolled for us. Tomorrow, or someday down the road, I was sure the pain would feel sharp, but this moment only felt like a flat and numbing relief.

When the sun has set, no candle can replace it.
—GEORGE R. R. MARTIN

The "breaking open" part was finished, and now I would begin the long and frightening journey of "falling apart," which would include the learning of a new word: Un-remembering, which, by the way, is very, very different from *forgetting*.

It would be years later before I realized that the greater loss that day for the community was the "marketplace of ideas." In a more sophisticated area, elected leadership would never have let that go. They might have let me go, but they would have never closed the doors on their Chamber of Commerce.

PART TWO

FALLING APART

I always knew I would turn a corner and run into this day, but I ain't prepared for it no-how.

—LOUISE MERIWETHER

Bottom Side Up

*The falling apart stage was characterized by the three emotions we experience in any loss: denial, bargaining, and anger.
Everyone keeps telling me that time heals all wounds, but no one can tell me what I'm supposed to do right now.... Even if I had all the time in the world, I still don't know what to do with this time right now.*
—NINA GUILBEAU, *TOO MANY SISTERS*

After the emotional closing of the Chamber, I arrived home to discover that my husband had already emotionally shut down from his own fresh hell of a two-days-earlier corporate execution. I always felt abandoned when he shut down, although I knew it wasn't anything personal. It was just how he rolled.

Still—talking over coffee was my style. Our different styles did not help the situation. Graciously and un-deliberately, he allowed me the opportunity to sit with him in the Florida Room in our handmade oak swing and stare in silence at the lake behind our house. Exhausted and too empty to comfort him, I was grateful for the silence. With little conversation, we alternated staring at the lake and sleeping right through the fourth of July holiday. It was how we chose to escape the pain and bewilderment of again being *Bottom Side Up*.

Over the course of the next few days, I felt that deep, restless, angry energy coming on—the one I have when I know there's going to be another one of those discussions between "me and God."

That's one good thing I've learned about God: He's not like an empty suit that runs away when things get tough. Nope, God will hang right in the saddle with you while you rant and rave and cry and scream and curse and beg. God lets you attempt to make deals with Him, slam things on the floor, burn your business cards, and think terrible thoughts about how to get revenge and inflict pain on those who have hurt you, deliberately or not. At least God is not a shrinking violet in the face of adversity.

Jerry, my good man husband, was much too reverent or perhaps too scared to question God about such matters. At least he would never do so out loud or even admit to it after the fact. He was uncomfortable with my questioning as well. So I tried to keep my open comments to a minimum in order not to offend him. In fact, Jerry never talked much at all about us being *Bottom Side Up* or how we got here or who was to blame or what strategies he thought might be available to us to try to get right side up again. I secretly wondered if his silence meant that he had just given up.

My birthday was a few days later—on July sixth. A few of my friends made dinner for me and forced me to come out. We had all had just finished reading the book *The Shack*, which was a popular Christian novel about how God manifests himself and his healing power through ordinary, everyday people. We discussed the book that night at dinner, trying not to talk about the awful things that had just happened to Jerry and me: losing our jobs on the same week and all—not to mention the fact that the very powerful Chamber of Commerce had just closed its doors. God forbid we would all talk about the very large elephants in the room.

Over dinner, birthday cake, a bottle of wine, and the discussion of *The Shack*, we pondered which one of us God might choose as the person through which he would speak. We decided it probably would be Jerry since he didn't drink and talked very little unless he had something profound to say.

I had a little too much wine with my birthday cake, and, of course, when Jerry and I got home that night, I was ready to talk. Jerry went straight to bed, and I climbed in beside him and started talking. Lying in bed beside him and referring to *The Shack*, I asked Jerry if he thought he might possibly be God because, if he was, I needed him to explain to me why all this bad stuff was happening to us. And, of course, the wine had kicked in and uncorked the tears that I had been holding back for days.

Actually, the scene was quite messy. Jerry very gruffly assured me that he indeed was not God, to which I replied, "Well I didn't think you probably were anyway, because why would you do this to yourself?" Just like Mama, he cautioned me about disrespecting God, especially while consuming wine.

I ignored his comment and continued to talk, reminding him that even though he had lost his job too, I was way worse off than he was. He had twenty-six years with his former company and a pension. His current company was still in business, so he had COBRA, and what did I have? A big fat nothing, except the fear that I was going to be personally saddled with some of the Chamber debt, especially the credit card debt—which turned out to be a well-founded fear. And the people who fired him weren't his friends like the people who fired me.

Finally, he spoke briefly of his own pain. "Linda, I had a career; you had a life and, might I remind you, it was one that you loved. I have a pension; you have a big flock of friends and a headful of front porch stories. And your friends might have fired you, but they still love you anyway."

I returned conversational fire: "What good are stories? I'll take the pension and COBRA any day."

And then he rolled over and went to sleep, leaving me to my feelings of abandonment again.

I was a farm girl, and I needed to work, doing something. So the next day, I bought some paint and started painting in the very back of the closet. It was the deep closet, the one right under the staircase—the closet that is designated as our "safe place" in storm emergencies. I chose that one on purpose because it seemed like I could just get way back in there and hide forever. That day, I hoped no one would find me—ever!

Painting was good for me. It was like staring, only with movement. It turned out that hiding was not that easy. I had been a community fixture for so long that almost everybody had my cell phone number. And after the fourth of July holiday when everybody woke up and realized that the Chamber had closed and I was gone, my phone started ringing. I let the voice mail collect the condolences, questions, and apologies. Someone said it was impossible. It was like an unsinkable ship had sunk.

But eventually, I had to answer my phone and do things like go to the grocery store. That's when I started to notice that there was a whole bunch of other people just like me who were *Bottom Side Up*. I recognized them right away because, obviously, they were the ones at the grocery store on Monday morning.

One day, I ran into a lady that I had known in my "before" life. In her other life, she always wore a business suit and usually pearls, and her makeup was always perfect. I never saw her hair out of place, even in the Florida humidity. She came over to me, wearing that kind of lost *Bottom-Side-Up* look, and shared that she had heard about what had happened to me and the Chamber, and she was so sorry. She just couldn't believe that the Chamber had closed.

"You put so much energy into the Chamber for so many years. You must be devastated." Then she quickly and meekly confided that she and her husband had just lost their jobs. She went on to say that they were going through such a tough time, and she thought she might have had a little miniature meltdown. She was just curious if anything like that might have happened to me.

I shared with her the story of my birthday meltdown, when I drank too much wine and asked my husband if he might be God. I also told her that I had been painting the back of the closet, and she finally laughed. I confided that indeed my meltdown had not been mini, and I did not think I was finished yet. The release of laughter also brought the release of her tears.

"Linda, we don't know what we're going to do."

"Neither do we," I replied. Instinctively, I hugged her. She asked if I had an e-mail address and if she could send me her resume in case I ran across something that might fit with her skills.

"Because," she said, "you know my talents as much as anyone."

I wanted to say, "Duh—the Chamber closed. Remember? I don't do job placement anymore." But in that moment, my own demise receded into the backdrop, and I gave her my personal e-mail address and promised I would keep my ear to the ground for her. Because it was true—I did know her skills as much as anyone, and now I also knew her pain as much as anyone.

Bottom Side Up

And mostly, I was blown away that she still believed in me, because I certainly didn't believe in myself anymore.

Bottom Side Up was indeed strange.

And that was how I got started listening to *Bottom-Side-Up* stories. I could have changed my phone number, but perhaps it assuaged my intense need be connected to the community and to my friends. And that was the day I realized that our need for belonging is almost as great as our need for money.

Back at the defunct Chamber, the "suits" were moving through the painful legal ordeal of shutting down the organization. They asked me to assist, which was fortunate for me as I surprisingly discovered that I was personally responsible for some of the debt of the organization. I was bewildered. The biggest issue was the chamber credit card. The Chamber attorney was negotiating the debt down on the card, but my personal credit score was going to take the hit. Luckily the "suits" turned out to be the decent people I thought they were. They sold enough assets to pay the debt in full. It was unthinkable to me that not only had I lost my job, but I also was about to get stuck personally with the debt of the organization. It happens to a lot of people—talk about *Bottom Side Up*!

As summer rolled on, the realization that the chamber was gone was beginning to sink in. Word got around town that you could call and talk to me about being *Bottom Side Up*. There were a lot of people losing jobs and homes and families. After all, I cussed and prayed and argued with God. I was unashamed of laughing or crying, so people felt pretty comfortable saying whatever they wanted to me. I had listened to their stories for over a decade. They said they still needed to know that I was around. I really think it just made them feel like they were still around. Perhaps I was flattered that they still thought about me because I was feeling like I had fallen into the abyss. Anyway, it seemed to work for all of us.

So here are excerpts from some of those *Bottom-Side-Up* questions that people asked me in their darkest days—and my answers on my darkest days.

Question (from a friend that lost his big CEO job):
"Linda, do you think it's crazy to feel all tangled up?"

Answer:
"Tangled up—that's a great description. Most of us feel that way. Angry, scared, sad, confused, bewildered, guilty, ashamed…tangled up. Don't try to make it pretty or sterile. You can't make a silk purse out of a sow's ear. (Remember that I was raised on a farm in Tennessee, and I revert to my native tongue when I'm under stress or hangin' out with my Tennessee friends.) Indeed, it is all very tangled up. It's raw and messy, and you are not going to know who the hell you are for the foreseeable future. This *Bottom-Side-Up* thing makes you feel disoriented—like having a very, very long bout of vertigo."

Question:
"Were you ever mad about the Chamber closing?"

Answer:
"Absolutely. Anger is a big part of it. The only thing that keeps you from throwing things and tearing off somebody's head is just that the angry days are punctuated by several days in a row of not having the energy to shave or shower or even get dressed. I suppose that the depression balances the anger, which is probably a good thing—although it doesn't feel that way."

Question (from someone who wants to know the shortcut):
"So how's the best way to get right side up again?"

Answer:
"Sorry, this isn't a McProblem; there is no 'drive thru.' It doesn't come with instructions or warnings. There is no chain of command, no policy, and no procedure manual. Begin wherever you are, and, by the way, you don't have to try to bounce back right away. I tried to get right back up and discovered that it was like trying to rebuild your house in the middle of a hurricane. You have to wait 'till the

wind stops howling. The storm is the storm. The wind stops blowing when the wind stops blowing. I know that's not what you wanted to hear. Tear the pages out of your old employee handbook, roll them up, make a paper house out of them, and then set the damn thing on fire, sweep up the ashes, put them in a bag, grab some beer or wine, go somewhere, and cast the ashes to the universe. Have yourself a good cry and then blame it on the alcohol. While you're at it, if you can muster the courage, go ahead and ask God, 'Why'" (He laughed and said, "Sounds like a plan.")

Question:
"Linda, do you ever miss things?"

Answer:
"All the time. My husband and his coworkers took turns taking doughnuts to work on Friday for twenty years. After the corporate executions, they stayed in touch by e-mail. They still assigned someone to bring virtual doughnuts. That person was in charge of e-mailing a picture of doughnuts to the group on Friday. They laughed about it, but I knew they were sad. They missed each other and called it doughnuts—whatever works. Me? I missed the damn keys to the building. Can you believe that? I know it's crazy, but that's what I kept missing. I felt like I had been locked out of my own world—like I had no control—and I'd have to sit on the doorstep of life, ringing the doorbell 'till somebody let me in. For all know there ain't even anybody at home—anywhere—anymore. I know God tells the preachers to tell us to 'knock, and the door shall be opened,' but I'm really more comfortable having the keys, just in case."

Question:
"Shame, Linda—did you ever feel ashamed?"
(This question was from a former business owner who tried to hide from me in a big-box store, where he ultimately found a job after losing his business, but the "big box" made him wear a red vest. He said he was ashamed for me to see him looking like Santa Clause.)

Answer:

"Listen to me, I've been ashamed plenty of times. I've had a panic attack dressed in high heels and a business suit. One night I showed up to a community event at the country club like I had done a thousand times. (Remember, I was a social butterfly.) I did what all the books say to do—reconnect, network, and get the word out that you are available for work. So, I got all dressed up for success, took a deep breath, and entered the fancy room at the country club. And then it happened: I started to get all sweaty, and my heart was racing because I imagined that everybody was looking at me. I thought they could see right through my business suit to my *Bottom-Side-Up*-ness. I could barely get my breath. I felt raw and naked, like the underside of my broken wings was totally exposed. I decided a glass of wine would help, so I got one. But it didn't. And because I get sick before I get drunk, I knew another glass of wine was not the answer. So I just quietly excused myself and exited the building. When I got outside, I took off my high heels and ran to my car as fast as I could. I really needed to get back to painting that closet.

"(That night it never entered my mind that they might actually be glad to see me or that they could possibly like me without a name badge. *Bottom Side Up* makes you imagine things.) Back in the safety of my car, I made a mental note to God: *I ain't doin' this some more.* And then I cried and informed Him that if he wanted to tell me anything, He could just make a house call, 'cause I wasn't coming out any time soon. That night, I finally claimed my grief and sadness and falling apartness and how it had changed me and made me afraid instead of bold and audacious. And dammit, I still so much missed the keys."

Shift Keeps Happening

In a few months, I landed a job as Community Relations Manager with a prestigious retirement community. One of my former executive board members was assistant director, which is probably why I got the job in the first place. My office was off campus in a strip plaza, and there was no one there except me. I was terribly isolated and lonely and still grieving the Chamber. The media still called me for "sense-making" of things, but I really couldn't speak anymore because I might say something my new employer didn't want me to say. The new role was very strange to me.

So I just became still and quiet. I felt like the dummy for a ventriloquist. My mouth was moving, but someone else was really doing the talking. I wasn't part of the "in crowd" or the strategic planning. I was just the dummy. I wanted to want to stay here in this space, learn to say nothing, and do as I was told. I was grateful for the job and the health insurance.

And then to add more *Bottom Side Up*-ness, Jerry's adult son, my stepson, lost his job, got a divorce, and moved in with us. He brought a cat. It might be appropriate to mention here that I'm not really comfortable around cats. It's nothing personal, but they make me itch.

To make matters worse, one day we smelled something right outside our front porch and noticed that the yard was wet. In my area of Florida, most of us are on septic tanks. Smelling something and seeing water can only mean one thing—a bad drain field, which can only lead to one other bad thing, which is spending a lot of money to replace it. And it just so happens that if the water table was up, or if you happened to live on a lake like we did, your front yard septic tank, under the new and improved regulations, had to be expanded 50 percent and mounded—that's right, mounded. You're required to have a very large crap mound right in your front yard. So now we own a house that is *Bottom Side Up*, with a crap mound in the front yard.

Too Many People—Not Enough House

Now stay with me here.. Things are getting really complicated. The community is in economic meltdown. Most of our real-estate assets (i.e., the American dream) are *Bottom Side Up*.

I've lost my dream job in a very public and embarrassing way. I have a job I'm grateful for, but it doesn't make me happy. My stepson and his cat have moved in. And I have a crap mound in my front yard.

But wait, there's more!

Our eight-year-old grandson, the one who struggles with ADHD and oppositional defiance disorder (which basically means he requires structure and constant cueing, but tells you no every time you remind him to do something) was being placed in a special class at school. The school constantly was calling his mom to either come for a conference or pick him up while she was trying desperately to keep her job. I pondered why a school system would be so insensitive to parents in such a time of crisis. The problem was that the system was in crisis too, which made the parents' crises so much worse. We all just blamed each other. (That happens a lot in *Bottom Side Up*, even from people who should know better.)

So we decided that since his dad had moved in, we would offer to take him for a few months and let his mom have a break. We thought we could give him more structure, regulate and decrease the twelve pills that he was taking every day for his behavioral issues, and let him go back home over the Christmas holidays. The task turned out to be not a task but another *Bottom-Side-Up* event.

The months rolled by. Things did not get better. Our grandson never went back home. We fell into the very chaotic world of children's mental health issues as well as an education system without the capacity to deal with children and families in a *Bottom-Side-Up* world.

Emotionally, our whole family was now *Bottom Side Up*. Our life had "fallen down around us," and then "we had fallen down around our life." When I watched the movie, *The Life of PI*, I knew exactly how PI felt when he got cast into a lifeboat with a bunch of zoo animals. We all simply did not know how to live together or to live in this very chaotic world into which we had been unknowingly thrust, almost overnight.

Bottom Side Up

Ships are safe in the harbor
But that's not what ships are made for.
—AUTHOR UNKNOWN

Though my home life was very complicated and I was still struggling with fatigue and dizziness, I was still working at my *J-O-B*. I missed my voice, the community, and myself terribly. It felt like I didn't belong anywhere.

At the end of January, not long before Groundhog Day, I was having one of those sleepless nights, which was pretty common. I took my pillow and electric blanket to my oak swing in the Florida room, the one where I can mark the passing of life by the rising and setting of the moon over the lake.

I lay in the handmade oak swing on that cold January night, wrapped in a blanket and mentally curled up in a question-mark ball, agonizing about what to do. Jerry woke up, missed me in the bed, and came to see about me. Startled, I looked up to find him standing over me in the cold Florida Room in his underwear, asking me what was I doing.

"I am praying," I said, "to any and all of the 'Holy Ones in Charge' that might be on call tonight. That includes God, Mother Mary, Jesus, the Holy Trinity, Allah, Buddha, Mother Teresa, Universe, Divine Spirit, and anyone else that pops into my head. I have also offered up respect to the mayor, although I want you to understand, I'm not praying to him. He can barely get a pothole fixed."

As usual, Jerry found no humor in the irreverent manner in which I was approaching life these days. I supposed he was like Mama, thinking I was going to keep on until I got both of us sent to hell. "What are you praying for?" he prodded.

"Change," I said, "just change. I'm in hell, and I think I've pitched a tent. I need to move on."

As usual, he muttered something under his breath about letting him know when I was going to get up so he wouldn't be worried. Then he just quietly waddled off in his underwear and went back to bed. As I already told you, *Bottom Side Up* makes people do strange things.

Linda S. White

The art of life lies in the constant readjustment to our surroundings.
—OKAKURA KAKUZO

A few days later, it was Groundhog Day. Jerry and I struggled every morning with the stressful and new routine of getting a very unwilling child to the bus stop. Exhausted from my new parenting responsibilities and feeling very displaced—like I was living somebody else's life—I would go to my new job.

That particular day, Groundhog Day, I was being moved from the shopping center office to the big gated campus. Behind the gates, I would have an office with no window. I'm claustrophobic, so the thought of spending the rest of my life in a windowless office made an uncomfortable knot in my stomach. I boxed up everything in the office (per instruction) and sat alone, waiting for the moving trucks.

I thought about my other life, the one where I was always solving some problem, and somebody was always waiting to see me. But now, I was the one who was waiting. I didn't like not being in control. The moving truck was supposed to arrive at 10:00 a.m., but at 10:30 a.m., my supervisor called to tell me that the move had been rescheduled for the afternoon. I went to lunch alone and pondered my life. Right after I got back to the office, my supervisor showed up to notify me that my community relations position was being phased out at the end of the month. I could stay or I was free to leave now, and they would pay me until the end of the month.

It was only a few nights ago that I had prayed for change. It looked to me like the prayer had worked, so I just hugged her and graciously thanked her for the opportunity. Then I just gave her my keys and drove off then and there into Groundhog Day. I wasn't going to have to go into the windowless office after all.

Of course, I didn't have any salary or insurance either.

Back at home, the place with the cat and the septic mound and all the people, I walked in the door, looked at Jerry, and said, "I just lost my job again."

"Oh no, what are you going to do?" he asked with a panicked look on his face.

"Take a nap," I replied. And I did.

Note to self: Don't ask all the spirits for something if you don't really want it.

And there I was, *Bottom Side Up*, and dammit, I had lost the keys again. One of the business managers in the area had showed me a trick he used while waiting for his corporate execution.

He prepared by keeping all of the facility keys on one key ring that was hooked to his personal keys by a key snap. He figured that when his moment came, he could just quickly unsnap the facility keys without too much thought, which is how I was able to give up the keys without much effort. I found out that losing the keys was a big deal to a lot of people—keys and the company phone.

That's where all your contacts are and the modern seat of your "sense of belonging," which is why I always kept my own personal phone.

Where Do I Belong?

The community people continued to call and share their *Bottom-Side-Up* stories. Most of them had no idea about what was going on in my life, and I never told them until now. I listen more than I talk. I never changed my cell number. So I'm guessing that their stories were important to me.

Question:

"Linda, did your body clock change?"

Answer:

"Absolutely—sleep all day, up all night. I belly laughed when people asked me if I ever felt strange when I woke up in the morning. In the beginning, I would get all showered and dressed for life, and I didn't even have a life—at least not one that I recognized. It was like showing up at the airport and them remembering that you had not even booked a flight. And then I would be exhausted from all the *Bottom*

Side Up-ness, so I just took a nap because sleeping can let you run so far away from all of it. Clinically, I guess they call that depression."

Question (from someone freshly plunged into *Bottom Side Up*-ness):
"What do you do with yourself all day?"

Answer:
I tried to watch morning TV. In my whole life, I had never watched morning TV. The TV ladies were all beautiful with teeth whitener and Botox and stilettos—perfect. On one particular morning, the discussion was about how to keep liquids like coffee or red wine from staining your teeth. They suggested that drinking coffee or wine from a straw could keep those delicious colored liquids from staining your teeth."

Note to self: I am not drinking coffee or wine through a damn straw. That's just silly.

So that ended my attempts to fill my day with TV. I clicked off the TV, poured a big cup of strong coffee, went out to my dock, watched the ducks paddle across the lake, and thought to myself: *What the hell is this world coming to?* (You talk to yourself a lot when no one else is listening.)

Question:
"Do you ever feel anxious in the late afternoon and night?"

Answer:
"Around 5:00 p.m., when nighttime started to set in, I would get that anxious feeling because it was time to go home, and I was already there. Everybody in the house was on edge and hungry. And, yes, I do understand why five o'clock is called "Happy Hour"—because it's a very stressful time. One of my friends also calls it 'arsenic hour.' She says you want to give everyone in the house arsenic because they act so crazy.

"And you want to know about bedtime? OMG, there's nothing worse than trying to sleep when you're *Bottom Side Up*. I would go to bed with a threesome: my husband, me, and my inner critic. And my inner critic loves to talk smack to me at night. 'Hi there, you probably ain't never gonna work again. Baby Doll, don't your car need new tires? Whatcha gonna do about health insurance? You gonna look funny wearing that fast food cap at your age. Hon, you can kiss that Italy trip good-bye. Whatcha gonna do tomorrow? Same thing as you did today?' followed by a wicked laugh. 'You and your whole family probably gonna end up starving to death.' And then the meanest thing would happen: he would get right inside my head and whisper 'you are a nobody; you don't even have any keys; and furthermore, you probably ain't never gonna get any more keys, ever again. Nobody would give you keys anyway, 'cause you suck.'

"But occasionally, I would find the courage to talk back. 'Hey you, Dipstick.' (That's what I call the inner critic if I'm feeling like my old self—a bit sassy.) 'If I can argue with God, surely I could find the courage to talk back to a Dipstick. I'm beginning to like these blue jeans. They be feeling damn good to me. I can go to yoga class now and paint and write and have a nap anytime I get ready and go to lunch with whomever I choose. And I have time to cook really scrumptious food instead of going through the drive thru.'

"And every now and then, I started to notice the beautiful colors of the sunset and the way the moon sparkled like a million diamonds across the lake right outside my back door. If this was where my story ended, perhaps I had landed in a not-so-bad place after all."

I began to see things that had always been here, but I had been too busy to notice. After a while, *Bottom Side Up*-ness makes you see things differently.

> *In a dark place, the eye begins to see.*
> —THEODORE ROETHKE

I have always had a cup of coffee around three o'clock in the afternoon, even in the hot Florida summers. It's my "Happy Hour." One afternoon, I pulled out my never-used French Press and boiled water for the coffee. As it steeped, I sat patiently inhaling the rich aroma of the freshly ground coffee beans, thinking about my life. And every now and then, I would be content in "Life's Waiting Room."

But I quickly learned that *Bottom Side Up* is not a position. It is a condition—a spiral condition, ever changing and very unpredictable.

Some days my hair was messy, and I didn't know if I ever even wanted any keys again. And then on other days, I so much wanted to fly again, fast and high, with my keys in my beak. And my heart would be sad, because I was afraid that my soul was so jaded and my wings so broken that they would never heal, and if they did, I would probably be too afraid to fly again anyway. Falling and hard landings make you afraid that way.

Question:
"Some days, I'm just so full of rage. Did you ever feel angry?"
(This question was from a computer engineer who had been out of work for almost two years.)

Answer:
"Absolutely, I've been angry. I stayed angry for months and months. I wanted to ride a horse without a pooper catcher right down the middle of the high-tech corridor, wearing a T-shirt that said, 'Life is Messy, you people in charge need to get working on it.' Anger is a phase; try not to get stuck there—not a good place to pitch a tent."

Question:
"Linda did you ever just wonder: *Why?*"

Answer:
"Jesus H. Christ, *yes!* I stayed curled in a mental question-mark ball, asking *why* for the longest time. In fact, I sometimes still do—although, not as often. I think it's just our nature to engage in 'sense making.' I asked *why* to just about everything."

But the truth is that I really don't know any more than the first time I asked.

Problems cannot be solved by using the same thoughts that created them.
—ALBERT EINSTEIN

After I started to see everything differently, I could see a few solutions to the problems of the economy. And I thought: *Wow, I've found the answers.* And since I wasn't part of a large organization and I was no longer bound by social props or the special business interests of a flock of six hundred businesses, I had even more options for finding solutions.

Hmm, this might actually work.

I could teach the community how to get out of *Bottom Side Up*. I didn't have to worry about protecting the "suits" or being fired by them or offending some special-interest group. I was free, and I could finally make a real difference. I could do some truth telling and some critical thinking, so I thought.

One morning, I picked up a colored pencil and started to draw in my art journal. It was a picture of a small wimpy flower that was pot-bound. I realized that I was awakening from a sleep. None of us could respond to the crisis upon us because we were pot-bound. We just needed to get a different pot.

So I started looking for another pot for my own life.

Theodore Rolkeln said, "In a dark time, the eye begins to see." That was exactly what was happening to me. It was as though I had started to fall awake. I saw government signs that had always been there, but I had never really seen them before.

They read:
NO PARKING
NO SWIMMING
NO SPITTING
NO PEDESTRIAN ACCESS
NO PUBLIC ACCESS

NO LOITERING
NO TRESPASSING

And I thought to myself: People, we need some *yeses* here. Why won't somebody tell us what we *can* do?

And I wanted to rent a skywriter airplane and have it write: "More singing, dancing, laughing, loving, holding on, letting go, having fun, taking risks, helping others, and starting over!

Dammit, everybody, just take some risks, be creative, and live out loud! Screw all the permits and fees and red tape. We are all up to our asses in alligators. We need to drain the swamp, here.

Note to government: Somebody very wise told me this, "You people in charge need more white out, less ink."

And then I realized that perhaps I might be growing through some of the tangled parts. I was beginning to see light again. But I was also becoming disenchanted with government. I blamed them for not being more responsive to what was happening. Maybe the government wasn't going to help us get right side up again after all.

So I Got Me a Bigger Pot

You may be wondering what I did next.

Well, I found a business partner—actually, the one who told me that government needs more white out and less ink—and we launched a little redevelopment and community engagement business. I loved his philosophy.

He was a general contractor and could see patterns in things that were amazing to me. He didn't give two hoots about politics and thought I was too attached to government. He said government made stupid rules. He knew what rules didn't work and how to make construction and development projects run smoother. He was so wise that I thought the government should just set him up in a teepee and come by and ask him how to kick start the economy and get a few people back working again. We really believed that we knew ways to fast forward the community through at least a little of the pain.

Bottom Side Up

So we leased and cleaned and renovated this really dirty little 1920 bungalow that had the most spirit in the world. It was in the same city where the now-defunct chamber had been. We called it "The Bungalow," and the name stuck with everybody.

I had read that creativity and group problem-solving skills increased in smaller more intimate spaces, so this space was ideal. We painted the walls the boldest colors, and then my business partner painted a large quote across one wall: "New ideas are easily born in nonconforming environments."

I moved in my old family farm table to use as a conference table. We had a way-cool sitting area, situated around a fireplace. It was the most wonderful, creative place to talk and plan and, as it turned out quite by accident, to heal.

We put out a few really innovative redevelopment proposals for community-based micro-development projects. These were small projects because anything larger was just not going to work in this still-failing economic environment.

We also put out proposals for some of the tougher issues: historic preservation, which was really important to the citizens in this small town; a commuter rail station; and even a homeless shelter.

I was really concerned about the economic impact of a new commuter rail project that was being built in central Florida and running through the western part of our county. Before the chamber closed, I had traveled to Portland to study their commuter rail system. I knew that for the system to be successful, there had to be some pretty dense development around the station. But development plans had come to a halt, and the chamber was not there to push the dialog.

My business partner and I tried to revive the plans by creating a plan that integrated the rail project as part of the ecotourism system along the St. Johns River. One night, we went before a city council to get them to pass a resolution supporting a commuter rail station in their city. They unanimously approved the project and set us on our way to work on getting it to Washington. The proposed station would be in close proximity to one of the most visited Florida state parks. It was home to a beautiful natural spring that invited snorkeling and canoeing as well as watching the beautiful endangered sea cows called manatees. There was a bicycle trail head close by. It would make our area a destination for ecotourism.

I wanted people to come to visit our area, not just leave it to work and spend their money some other place and come home to sleep. It seemed as though there were so few of us that really could see the beauty and opportunity of our area. I was happy that the city council was supportive of the project. But the last thing they did that evening was fire the city manager. And dammit, I knew we were *Bottom Side Up* again.

I had a knot in my stomach because I had lost the leader that understood the project and the community. They would find another manager, but I was pretty sure that whoever it was wasn't going to love or understand our community like all of us had. And I was right.

They hired a new female manager from someplace else—someone who would manage the corporation but not love the community. She had never been a city manager before, and I could see the writing on the wall. She was going to create her own dynasty, and none of us were going to be part of it. Our plans got sent to the round file as soon as she got behind her desk.

Some You Win; Some You Lose; and Some Just Get Rained Out

I had developed a community engagement platform, utilizing the style of a community planner named Wendy Sarkissian. She was an urban planner who had become disenchanted with the outcomes that were being created and set out on a journey to develop a new system for engaging communities in their futures. Her work was citizen driven, tough and tender, nurturing and heartfelt. She leaned deeply into the communities and engaged them to identify and solve tough social and community problems. I wanted her work style to be the guiding principle of my new company. Both my business partner and I wanted the community engagement to come from the bottom up—not from the top down. We wanted the community to be participants—not spectators.

My new work was exciting, and for the first time in a while, I was happy. I thought I had finally found another place where my work could be meaningful. The Bungalow was in sight of the historic city hall in the city I had always loved, the place where I could hear the city hall clock chime every hour—the place that charmed my heart.

My partner had a key made for me for the front door of The Bungalow. He made it red, white, and blue so that I wouldn't get it mixed up with my other keys. I immediately put it on my key ring, and when I unlocked the door for the first time, I smiled and said to myself: *Damn, this is great. I got the keys back and no one is ever going to take these away from me.*

And then, doing just like the inspirational books suggest—"Leap and the net will appear."—we leaped! And sure enough, we eventually fell flat on our asses. Actually, we were politically knocked on our asses. Excuse me, the politically correct phrase would be "with all due respect, the net did not appear."

Every three weeks, we gathered a community group together to discuss local issues and exchange information. We were developing the platform for the community-engagement model for our company, using an informal community-driven style. Some weeks, we would have as many as forty people in the room.

We gave the group a name, "Partners for Progress," because we all have the need to "belong," especially when things are *Bottom Side Up*. The group was made up of residents and business leaders and faith-based organizations. Black, white, conservatives, and liberals—they all came together for a common goal. They wanted to participate in community decision-making. It seemed to give them a sense of control when everything was so unstable. The group paid no dues and had no hierarchy. We had a facilitator and a "note taker" (because everyone wants their story to be retold).

My business partner was considered the facilitator. People loved him because he didn't say much. He just made sure everybody else got to talk. Clearly, he understood how to empower people. We opened our meetings by asking people to tell why they chose to live in this town, and the stories we heard were beautiful. The storytelling seemed to cause an "aligning" of sorts within the group. We asked people what they cherished, what they loved, and what they didn't love so much. From those meetings, we knew what was important to the community and set out to create and move initiatives forward that came from the people.

One night, after discussing the installation of red-light cameras, one of the "no-holds-barred" business people told me after the meeting, "Linda, that's bullshit about doing this for the safety of the people. They're just trying to feed HAL."

"Who's Hal?" I prodded. I didn't know anybody in City Hall by that name.

He reminded me about the old TV series, *Space Odyssey,* where the computer, Hal, was always telling everybody what to do because he was supposedly the smart one, and he was keeping the people safe. But in reality, it wasn't about the people, it was all about HAL.

He recalled one episode where the people were trying to conserve energy, and HAL told them that they would all die if they didn't make the spaceship cooler. The truth was: Hal was just hot.

We laughed every time the city raised fees or taxes, telling us we had to do it for the good of the people. We just called it, "Feeding HAL." (I still do)

And now you know who HAL is—the Government.

Many of the people who showed up to the community meetings later showed up at The Bungalow to share their *Bottom-Side-Up* stories, telling us how they were losing their homes and their businesses. We helped some of them find rental property if they were losing their homes. But there was really not much we could do, especially with a new city manager who wanted us all to sleep for two years until she could catch up.

One day in the summer, a long-time worker for the City (who knew she was losing her job) called and asked if she could come to The Bungalow to talk. The Bungalow had a cozy little kitchen nook where most people wanted to sit when they told their *Bottom-Side-Up* stories. That was where I had positioned our conference table, which was my old family farm table. I tried to make sure I had comfort foods on hand for such occasions. Ice cream was my choice for that day.

When the city employee arrived, I could tell she was devastated. We were in eyesight of the City Hall, so she walked, not wanting anyone to see her car at The Bungalow. She knew she was losing her job, although she hadn't been officially notified. As predicted, the manager would sentence almost all the upper-level managers who were there before her to a corporate execution.

We talked for an hour, and I tried to help this wonderful woman put some sort of plan in place for when her job ended. She thought it might be as early as the end of that week.

As did most people, she left a resume with us—in case we heard of a job opening. As she was leaving, she thanked me, and instinctively, as I did to almost everyone, I reached out to hug her. Laying her head on my shoulder, she started to cry. I was wearing a sleeveless blouse that day, and I could feel one of her tears rolling down my bare arm. It broke my heart and made me angry that she had to go through this. I reassured her that no matter what was said to her, she had done a great job. In all the years that I had known her, she had loved her community and had made it a better place. She had to believe that, and she had to keep believing in herself. The community had loved her, and some new person coming to town couldn't change history. She might change the future, but the past was ours and the memories that go with it.

By chance, I had a meeting scheduled with the new city manager within the hour that very day. I was not going to be in the mood for her condescending attitude. We had presented our first proposal for historical and heritage preservation to her a few weeks earlier. I think that might have been the day that I started doubting the city-manager form of government, something that I had previously believed in very strongly.

It seemed like leadership inside the city halls was like musical chairs. Nobody ever stayed for long. How would we ever move a community forward under this scenario? Don't get me wrong, I still know some really great managers, but many of the good ones are sitting on the bench.

So, back to the new manager: she said that since she had just gotten here, and since she wasn't from around here, she had no idea what was going on, except that she had concerns about a plan that had been developed by citizens and regular people like us. She explained that she wanted to bring in a large, professional consulting company. Perhaps we could revisit our plans in two years.

I tended to disagree that a twenty-five-year general contractor and a Chamber Chief with fifteen years of community and economic-development experience were just regular people. And so, with all due respect, I replied, "Well, we don't have a couple of years. Do you really just expect us to tell these people who have been meeting for months, giving input to a plan about their own community while also trying to hang on to their homes and businesses, to just go home and sit quietly for two years while you catch up?"

The unemployment rate was in the top tier in the nation, hovering officially at about 12.5 percent. In reality, we believed it to be much higher because of the number of self-employed people and the foreclosure rates in our area. The foreclosure rates were the fourth highest in the nation, and there were so many homeless children right in the shadow of the Big Mouse, and she wanted us to wait two years—*really?*

I was righteously indignant. I had already seen more than my share of pain in this community.

I did not want to bear one more day of sitting idly by, listening to stories of another foreclosure or seeing one more homeless family or one more closed business or hearing about one more suicide. I was completely blown away by her indifference to the suffering of the community and even what I perceived to be a disdain for the citizens and the community she served.

It wasn't long before the city staff was no longer allowed to meet with us in our monthly community meetings to discuss issues and exchange information. We were very rapidly losing the civic capacity that had propelled this community to success in the prior decade. And then I realized that we had fallen awake, but she and so many others were still sleeping. Therefore, the word *zombie* became self-explanatory to me.

Later, after another couple of other innovative project proposals, I had the pleasure of meeting with her again. I asked her straight up why none of my proposals could even get consideration. I reminded her that I was a female who had a locally owned business with a successful track record of economic and community development. She just looked at me and said that I didn't have political support from some of the county's elected officials.

"So you'll let this community suffer for that?" I asked.

She never answered the question. And, dammit, I knew I was still *Bottom Side Up*.

The politics of my broken spirit were deepened by the fact that we were all women. And I realized the painful truth that even in the middle of the worst economic times since the great depression, public officials, especially women, my own kind, would ignore human and community needs in favor of power and politically expedient decisions—and possibly even revenge. The conflicts and disappointments within me tore me apart.

There would be no more "we the people." There would be no more collective problem solving and no more social progress in this beautiful little community. What I knew then (and believe even more now) is that civic capacity—which helps to solve community problems—begins in the hearts of the public officials. We had lost the connection of the people to their government. Without heart, there is no connection, and without connection from people to their government or their community, there can be no resilience in the face of stress. It made me angry and very, very sad.

So I just went back to The Bungalow, opened the door with my keys, made a strong pot of coffee, and tried to process what was happening to me. We were women, and we were supposed to raise each other up, and yet, the opposite was happening—and it was happening on purpose. It was something I just could not understand.

Putting myself aside, the community deserved better than this. Somehow, I felt strangely like a paragraph from *Catcher in the Rye*. I felt as though I had been catching the dreams and the pain of the community, giving voice to their needs for years. I had been their catcher. But now, I was powerless. They would have to either find a new voice or go on without one. There was little else that I could do. It was a reality that I had to accept.

People parted, years passed, they met again—and the meeting proved no reunion, offered no warm memories, only the acid knowledge that time had passed and things weren't as bright or attractive as they had been.
—VALLEY OF THE DOLLS

So I swallowed my pride and called Sage, thinking that maybe she would help me try to do something for the community. I asked her if she would have breakfast with me. Surprisingly, she said yes. And I took her some fresh rosemary out of my garden just like I used to do when we were BFFs, because she loved to roast fresh rosemary in her chicken. I guess I was thinking it might be a peace offering.

After a few minutes of cocktail talk, I told her that I had been told that by the new city manager that none of my projects would be approved because I was on the wrong side of the political power base. "After all, I am a business woman, and I live in your district, and these projects are the kinds of projects you support. These projects are important to the community."

She just politely and powerfully looked me straight in the eye and, without so much as a blink, said, "Well, you are on the wrong side of the political power base."

And in that moment, a light came on. For the first time, I understood that our community (and probably most communities) had become a political chess game of moves and countermoves, especially since the economic meltdown. My only solace was that I once heard a quote: "at the end of the game, pawns and kings all go back in the same box." There really wasn't much else to say. I told her that I was tired of fighting, and that no one in the community wins when we fight. She agreed.

We finished our breakfast with cocktail talk, and I said, "I hope you enjoy the rosemary." And she said, "Thank you; I'm sure the chicken will be delicious."

Driving away, I knew none of my projects would get approved. But I just didn't have the strength to fight anymore. It wasn't worth it. I was looking for friends, not enemies. I wished that we could be like we used to be, and that I could share the stories of the pain that I had seen. She had the political power to make a difference.

But then, I was on the wrong side of the political power base.

And sure enough, all my proposals just got shit-canned, and the city government brought in a big out-of-town consulting firm that had a PowerPoint presentation that would just "poof" away all the ugliness of a community. They could magically erase all of the overhead power lines and overlay buildings right next to the electronically created tree-lined streets, which, by the way, is entirely different from really planting the trees. And then the town you grew up in and married your true love in and raised your babies in and buried your parents in and walked in the sun and the rain and the moonlight in could look exactly like somewhere else—a place you didn't even know, a place you "unremembered."

Almost every day, I would take a walk down the street around my little 1920 bungalow, and the anger and sadness washed over me like an ocean wave. I wasn't really sad so much for me as I was for the people that loved this charming little place, the place where I used to take brides to sit on the beautiful winding oak staircase in city hall for their wedding photos.

I looked at all the huge old trees and the turn-of-the-century homes. This place was tired, and the economy had taken its toll, but it had such good bones and a joyful spirit. I was sad because I now knew that I would have to leave. This place would be just like having Alzheimer's disease:

some of us who loved it would remember it, but it would not remember us.

The manager was from someplace else, and she had convinced the elected officials that their town was ugly and needed radical renovation. The truth was, it was all about raising the tax base through destroying the old and bringing in new development and impact fees. Not that I'm against redevelopment. I just think it shouldn't destroy everything that is cherished by the community to increase the tax base to feed the government (HAL).

I thought back to how the community had shared with me what they cherished and wanted to keep and the new things they wanted to build. They wanted progress. They just wanted to be part of it.

I held their wishes and dreams in my mind, but the new manager had convinced the community and the elected officials that my company didn't know anything about redevelopment or historical preservation. What she had really convinced them was that the citizens didn't know anything because my redevelopment plan was created by their dreams and the things they cherished. These were now the things they were willing to walk away from and let a bunch of high-paid strangers tell them what they should and shouldn't like.

Their dreams were awesome, and they didn't even know it. I believed in the kind of leadership shown by our district congressman after September 11, when he personally called directly into his communities, engaging them and challenging them to participate in restoring the spirit of America. I wondered what difference that kind of leadership might have made to the local communities during the economic crash. I might have been an idealist, but I had actually seen it in real life, so I knew that it existed.

The thing about democracy, beloveds, is that it's not neat, orderly, or quiet.
MOLLY IVINS

I just stayed to myself for a while, curled up in The Bungalow in a question-mark ball and tried to understand *why*.

Bottom Side Up

I never did.

Back at home, I was still begging Jerry to move. He wouldn't even discuss the possibility with me. He said, "Linda, there will be people just like them some other place too."

I didn't think so, but maybe he was right.

One day, I got a call from the current mayor, inviting me to a community engagement meeting with the big "male-owned, out-of-town consulting company" to see their PowerPoint presentation. He said the "big company" was really good because my way—getting the people all involved—was just a lot messier.

"Damn straight, Mayor. my way is messy. I designed it that way. It's my brand." I guess he never read the quote by Molly Ivins: "The thing about democracy, beloveds, is that it's not neat, orderly. or quiet."

So my partner and I went to the "community visioning workshop." The process from the big out-of-town company was very familiar to me—just like at the airport: we stood in line to check in, and then we went to our seats, which were all lined up in neat rows. Then the city manager (i.e., hostess) welcomed us and directed our attention to the exit areas and the restrooms.

Next, the pilot (i.e., mayor) said, "Thanks for flying with us this evening. Just sit back in your seat and enjoy the ride."

Then they passed out our sodas and peanuts. Next, the "Big Consultants" turned on the awesome PowerPoint presentation and showed us this great new city that they had imagined. I said to my partner, "See I told you: Alzheimer City. It has almost no memories of any of us.

It has been stripped of all its charm."

We seemed to be the only ones who were disturbed. But that was because we had already fallen awake. The citizens ate their snacks and applauded at the end. No one asked how much it cost or how difficult it would be or what would happen to the existing businesses. Most of them just commented that the snacks were delicious.

And I just looked at my partner and whispered to him, "Dammit, there is something so wrong with us."

When I went to my car that night, I felt empty—not the way I felt after our community meetings, the messy ones where all the people talked. After those meetings, I felt energized and happy. We lingered under the moonlight and imagined what it would be like to see this little town glowing under the night sky with the business landscape restored with period street lamps. The citizens in our group had even given it a name and a spelling: "Ole Town." They told stories about what it was like to grow up here and who fell in love with whom and why they wanted to raise their children—and now their grandchildren—here. It was so beautifully messy—just the way people are. No one at our meetings ever talked about the snacks.

I loved the messy stories of real people and their lives, and I loved working at the edges and writing in the margins and helping people make their own lives better. I loved participators better than spectators. And at that moment, I hoped I would never have to go back into the box—the safe office with the white walls—even if I never got to work in the community again.

2010

Back at home, we were still undergoing huge shifts. I was trying to come to terms with having all these new men in my house: a grandson, an adult stepson with a cat, and a retired husband. There seemed to be no space for me anywhere. There was "men stuff" everywhere.

We tolerated each other, but not well. It was a very awkward dance. Neat was not their specialty.

They messed up so many drinking glasses every day that I finally packed away all of the drinking glasses except four—one for each person, thinking that they would wash their glass out when they drank out of it and put it away. But alas, I left some crystal candle holders on the top shelf of the dish cabinet, and they just got them down and made drinking glasses out of the candle holders.

It was so funny; I just let them drink out of them. It was a battle I was not going to win.

Question:

"How did you keep on going in the face of continued change?"

Answer:

"Well, some days you have to listen to bad-ass songs that give you courage to keep leaping. Mine was a country song called, "If You're Going through Hell, Keep on Goin'." If you don't have a bad-ass song, get one and load it on your iPod because, let me assure you, you are going to need one before this thing is over.

"One day an elected official of this little town that I so adored showed up at The Bungalow. He had a cup of coffee and looked around at The Bungalow and said, 'Well, this old thing needs to be torn down. The windows are all crooked and messy.' I could sense that they were already mentally preparing to implement their new redevelopment plan.

"And I said, 'So is life, and that's the beauty of it all. There is memory and mystery here.

Your millions of dollars big-old-consultant redevelopment plan looks like a sad city with an extremely bad case of amnesia. When y'all are through with it, your community won't remember who it was or the things it loved or what made it feel special and authentic. It can't even remember its own story. And you just support tearing everything down and building back an amnesia city. That's just crap, in my opinion. And you never ask anybody who lives here what they really want or think. The citizens here will be disconnected, and they won't even know why. None of you will.'

"I guess he never understood the story of the *Velveteen Rabbit.* (Read it if you never have.) And then I felt sorry for him. But he was in charge, and I wasn't, and then I felt sorry for me and sorry for the people because I knew they had lost their voice. And the people who governed them now said they knew what the people needed. It was really all about what HAL needed. This awakening that 'HAL' no longer cared about what the people wanted made me very sad. The new breed read magazines from someplace else, and they stopped engaging their own people. They were beginning to feel the effects of the downturned economy, and now they were focused on how to feed HAL. All of the community-based groups were gone—starved and regulated out by people who wanted complete power and control. The silence of the community was loud.

MORE FAMILY SHIFT

As I mentioned before, our grandson (who has ADHD and oppositional defiance) had come to live with us. Unable to function without constant cueing, encouragement, and supervision, we made the choice to change our lives forever and take him to live with us permanently, hoping to try to give him one small chance to grow up to be a good man. The universe had handed us more shift.

How could I claim to have compassion for the world if it didn't start with my own family?

> *Sometimes you have to claim something, even if it is just your own confusion.*
> *--Author Unknown*

Not only was I having to rethink everything I knew about community and government, I also had to relearn so many things about children. One of them was how to tell bedtime stories.

One night, I tucked my grandson in real tight like he was a caterpillar in a cocoon. I told him that when he went to sleep, he would grow butterfly wings, and then he would be free to kick off the covers and fly anywhere he wanted.

Through sleepy eyes he asked, "Nana, how long does it take to grow butterfly wings?"

"It all depends on what kind of butterfly you become. I think if you want to become a spectacular butterfly, it takes a while." I rubbed his head until he drifted off to sleep. I wished I could always keep him this safe. But his world was *Bottom Side Up* too, and nothing is safe or easy in *Bottom Side Up*—even for children.

The Collar and the Glass

Back in the community, things were growing progressively worse. The meltdown was now affecting everything. People were constantly calling me, wanting to talk about what was happening to them. They wanted to get my perspective on what was going on and how long I thought it was going to last. The truth was that I had no idea.

One morning, I got a call from a local pastor who asked if I could meet for lunch. It was an unusual call, and I could sense the urgency in his voice. He chose the restaurant and was already there when I arrived. He had discreetly requested a scotch on the rocks, and I knew this was going to be a serious conversation.

We exchanged pleasantries until after the scotch kicked in, and, looking down into the glass, he began to speak, "How does it feel when they betray you? How does it feel to be pushed away from something you built at the hands of people you served? How does the end feel? I know you know."

I knew he was trying to prepare for the end of his long tenure at his troubled church, the one that he had built from nothing. He had shepherded the congregation for almost twenty years. He had married them, preached their funerals, baptized their wretched souls, christened their babies, and given them the bread of the Lord Jesus Christ's body during the communion. But now, that was not enough in the "what-have-you-done-for-me-lately scenario."

I gently laid my hand on his arm. It always seemed like I was touching everybody. I knew it wasn't politically correct, but I did it anyway, and besides, nobody seemed to mind. I answered compassionately, "I don't know why people do what they do. They crucified Jesus Christ and fired Lee Iacocca. I'm guessing that firing a pastor and a chamber chief during an economic meltdown isn't all that hard."

Humbled that he would share his pain so openly with me, that he trusted me enough to drink scotch in front of me, I prodded him to go deeper. "You seem certain of the outcome already."

Ironically, as he raised the glass for another sip of scotch, I could see his cleric collar through the rim of the scotch glass. The image was branded in my mind. *Bottom Side Up* and betrayal do strange things to people.

He said that the church members only wanted to be entertained. He bemoaned that they had so many services and cantatas and celebrations that he was so overwhelmed and exhausted he could no longer even hear God over the unrelenting, unquenchable, and selfish entertainment needs of his congregation. They had made him accountable for serving their every need, while the offerings were also drying up.

I told him of the pain I had felt as my own business flock required more than I could give, and then they wanted it for free, mostly because they were in financial straits themselves.

We both believed that the people who you trust the most are usually the ones who betray you—thus, the term *betrayal*. (You can't be betrayed by someone you don't trust anyway.) I told him that it wasn't his fault, that this damned economy made good people do bad things, and that I thought his faith would see him through.

He laughed and said, "Linda, I'm having a drink and talking to you. Obviously, faith is not working all that well for me today. I get paid to have faith. It's helpful for me to see it in you, someone who doesn't get paid to have it."

I smiled.

We finished lunch, and I thanked him for sharing his story. I told him that he could call me anytime. And then I hugged him. "It's hard. It takes some getting used to. I'm sure you'll find a new church where you can start over. You'll find another congregation where you're not under fire; the economy will get better; and the smile will come back to your heart."

Shaking his head, he offered, "Our house is *Bottom Side Up*; I don't know how we could move."

He had a point. It was an issue for most of us in the sun belt. My heart was heavy for him as I went back to The Bungalow.

The Bungalow had become a business office with unintended consequences, a place to just *be*, without a title or a business card. It had become a haven from the storms of life where we could come and sit with our pain, safe from the raging economic and personal storms that surrounded us, even if only for a few hours. I got very good at sitting with others during their "passages." It felt tender and vulnerable and sometimes awkward. It was a place where I did not try to fix others. Here, I had created, quite by accident, a safe place that allowed them (and me) to explore their (our) own open psychological wounds and raw edges—a place where only spirit can enter and glue back the broken pieces into something different. It was a place that I had to find by myself but also a place that I was happy to share with others. The Bungalow was a place where one could enter without a name badge or a business card, drink a cup of coffee or a glass of wine, and tell their story—the raw version, not the press release. A cast of characters showed up every day. Somehow they had learned of this place called The Bungalow, situated within a stone's throw of the city hall where I had once worked, a place that I would have to learn to "Unremember."

Their stories were memorable and haunting.

One day, a gentleman from our "before" life came by just to "pick my brain," he said. But I soon learned that he, like a lot of the others, really wanted to pick my heart. He sat at the (conference table) old farm table from my family, the place where everybody wanted to sit—the same table that Mama and Daddy and all of my family had sat around, pondering life for so many years. It was all I had left of them. That table knew a lot of stories.

We engaged in a bit of cocktail talk. The day was hot, and I offered him a bowl of ice cream, which was The Bungalow comfort food of choice that day. He had been the operations manager of a very large and powerful corporation before he went *Bottom Side Up*. I hoped the simplicity of a bowl of ice cream wouldn't offend him.

"That would be so great," he said as he smiled. Caressing the ice cream bowl in his hand, he began to eat and talk. He told the saddest story about his last days at the corporation, which by now had been well over a year ago. He was the one who had been assigned to carry out the "corporate executions" on his long-time friends and coworkers. That duty would be assigned to him until it was time for his own execution.

The story he shared that most haunted him (and obviously haunted me) was the "corporate execution" of a woman who had worked with him for fifteen years. She was a beloved fixture in the organization and had recently been diagnosed with a degenerative muscle disease. And then one day her name appeared on his corporate execution list. Agonizing over how he would tell her, he said he hated the organization that day, but he also hated himself. How would she cover health-care costs? She would not be able to get another job. He wondered how life could be so cruel and unfair. She would be devastated. Anticipating her reaction, he decided that he would ask her to attend a meeting with him on that fateful Friday afternoon.

Once in the car, he would tell her as directly and gently as he could. Then he would drive her until she stopped sobbing and got herself together enough to gather her personal belongings from the workplace, which he already had arranged to be respectfully placed in a box by someone in the organization who loved her.

And that was the way the "execution" rolled. As he had expected, she had sobbed uncontrollably and he had driven for almost an hour. He had encouraged her to cry and to say anything she wanted to say. He told the story without blinking, as if it were so horrible that he had stripped it of all emotion. I finished my ice cream with tears streaming down my face, for I knew the rest of the story.

She had died a few months before this conversation, around a year after her corporate execution. He said they named her illness as the cause of her death, but he knew that she died of a broken heart. I told him how lucky she had been to have had him as a boss and a friend.

He wished he could have done more.

I tried to console him. "I'm so sorry you had to go through that. You did all you could and more than most."

He finished his ice cream, wondering out loud whether his wife would continue to love him without his big job and his big title. I assured him that she would—that he was not his job. But he had to give it some time, and it wouldn't be easy. I knew how hard it was for Jerry and I to renegotiate the terms of our life with two boys and a cat. It's hard. *Bottom Side Up* is very, very hard.

And it was in the encouragement of others that I also tended to my own grief as I listened to story after story. My friend, former vice mayor and general contractor Greg, said that The Bungalow was a sanctuary, and anyone who was allowed inside received a rare gift—a soft place to land.

He too had lost his job—several of them, as a matter of fact—plus a failed election campaign. Sometimes I would throw dinner parties in The Bungalow, and Greg (who loved to cook) would always bring a dish. His Italian meatloaf was my favorite. I had always known him in the professional and political way until The Bungalow, where he would sit and talk politics and sometimes even tell his own personal stories.

"It's safe in here," he said.

Looking back, I now wonder if he knew that he was living his last days. He died suddenly after an upper respiratory infection, collapsing in the doorway of his home, waiting for the ambulance. He had left a message on my voice mail: "I don't feel good. Call me; I need a Linda fix." That usually meant that he wanted to tell me a joke or talk politics. By the time I returned his call, the sand had already run out of his hourglass. Life is so brief and fragile. I never even got to say good-bye.

2011

Hope Is Still a Strategy

Even though my business partner and I had met and interviewed dozens upon dozens of business people, asking them what they needed to stay in business, and had put out proposal after proposal to address their issues, no work had come. We had anecdotal information from the street that elected and public officials should have been beating the door down to get their hands on. We knew exactly what was going on in the business community and what regulations needed to be lifted to be able to keep just a small trickle of cash flowing in the local economy. Perhaps it was relaxing a sign ordinance or giving a grant to replace a sign under the new standards. The regulations were so complex that no business wanted to spend the kind of money that was required to meet the regulations, especially in such an uncertain economy.

Slowly, even the ones who had the money to keep going just gave up. Every day, there was another dark building. But the government (HAL) didn't seem at all interested.

One city manager said to me, "Why would I need that information?"

I thought to myself: *If you don't know, there's no point in trying to tell you.* But I just graciously thanked her for her time and left. It seemed as though she couldn't understand why I was even there.

It was becoming painfully clear to me that I would have to give up The Bungalow. It didn't make financial sense, even if my heart wanted to hang out here forever. We had leased and renovated The Bungalow with the intention of having an office for our community engagement and redevelopment business. Instead, it had emerged as something I could have never imagined—a place rich with stories and dreams, a place where people would take off their masks and share what it meant to be human. Everybody was in some stage of transition. Many were going through difficult passages. The Bungalow had emerged as an unintended consequence of a failed business initiative, a "touch point" for a lost community in search of meaning—perhaps a "touch point" for me.

At the height of the 2011 election season, candidate after candidate took refuge in the Bungalow. Some were running for state house of representative seats; some running for senate; some, running for local city council and county commission seats. The local partisan political clubs had splintered that year, and The Bungalow had become an alternative. It was transformed into a multi-campaign headquarters of sorts.

There were campaign signs and supplies and changes of clothes—especially for the state seats. There were dinner parties that spilled out into the street. Energy and ideas flowed like water. We operated as a "think tank," connecting people and aligning ideas.

I passed out water and coffee, cookies and ice cream, and an occasional glass of wine or scotch on the rocks, along with encouragement and nudges to keep going when energy waned. Most that hung out at The Bungalow won their elections. At least I was doing something right. It wasn't the thing I had planned, but I was working, and I had energetic people around me. And mostly, I had hope. Because as you know, one thing a farm girl likes to do is work.

One of them who won a republican house of representatives seat was insistent that I come on his staff. We had gotten used to each other in the campaign, and he knew how much I loved the community. He trusted me, and trust was no small thing to me.

Bottom Side Up

After the elections, I knew I would have to redefine my company again anyway. I didn't think much had changed in the community. The economy was still terrible, and the governments were hunkered down, trying to figure out how to feed HAL. Identifying community problems and creating solutions-oriented proposals made me happy. Not being able to get my proposals approved was bewildering to me. I had a female-owned business, and I couldn't even get a small contract in my own community, a community with no chamber of commerce. I couldn't understand.

So I decided to take a break and go to work for the state representative. I would be running the local legislative office. There, I would have enough power to get things done for people in the community. I intended to keep The Bungalow and my business. I would work part time, writing proposals, and my partner would take a more visible role. The legislative terms were only two years.

Maybe by that time, the economy would be better, and there would be other opportunities. Maybe I wouldn't be on the wrong side of the political power base by then. I so much wanted to run my own business. It was great not having to get approval from a board of directors. My partner and I ran things the way we wanted to in The Bungalow.

But he was used to that. A true entrepreneur and a conservative, he had worked for himself for thirty years, and I was learning a lot from him.

That year was going to be an epic legislative year. The community democrats (my own kind) were the ones who had orchestrated pulling a lot of the funding from the chamber, and I was still mad about that. It seemed ironic that I was now going to be part of the republican administration. Perhaps that's what drove me to the other side.

In the legislative office, I didn't have to make many decisions. In fact, I was not allowed to make many decisions. The furniture was standard issue; although, I was allowed to position it the way I wanted.

The state was very conservative. I purchased office supplies online, but I didn't have a lot of choice. There was a pretty lengthy policy-and-procedures manual. Lots of record keeping, logs, and documentation, CYA stuff—I was bored already.

Florida had elected a new republican governor. Education and pension reform were going to be the hot topics. The governor called the legislators to Tallahassee right after the new year to watch the movie *Waiting for Superman*. It was the first time I had a glimpse of what was happening in the education system. I didn't know that things were in such chaos. (That would become important to me as we were now raising an eight-year-old.)

My boss, the state legislator, was a maverick—brilliant and untethered. He went to Tallahassee with every intention of taking on the union and pension reform. I urged him to take it slow. Of course, he didn't. That's the way he rolls.

One of the things I liked about him was his boundless energy and the fact that he always told the truth, even when it wasn't popular. He was a freshman lawmaker who rolled out a pension reform bill, even before the legislative session began. In case you're not familiar with politics, that's pretty damn bold. During the beginning of the legislative session, I came to understand the word *cyber-attack* and the power of social media. I came to understand how they "twittered down Tunisia." The unions all over the state jammed our phone lines and shut down our e-mail. They intimidated us with threats. There was an uprising in Egypt at the time, and some of the callers threatened, "We're going to go 'all up Egypt' on your sorry asses." At least I wasn't bored anymore.

The process and the politics and the impacts of social media intrigued me, but it was mentally exhausting. The threats got pretty rough, and I was instructed to file a report with the local authorities, just in case.

It seemed strange to have to be protected by some of the same people whose union reps were sending in the threats. I'm just sayin'.....

Our office was picketed, and a couple of times, I found death cards by my car. I wasn't really afraid; however, I did look over my shoulder a lot. That was during the time that Arizona Congresswoman Gabrielle

Giffords had been shot at a constituent meeting, so we were all a little on edge anyway.

> *The privilege of a lifetime is being who you are.*
> —JOSEPH CAMPBELL

Something was haunting me, and it wasn't the nasty politics. I was used to that. In Florida, the speaker of the house makes most of the policies regarding the legislative offices. The policy dictated that I quit all community boards and get special permission from Mr. Speaker to be able to sit on any community boards. Additionally, I was going to have to give up my business.

I was none too happy about this rule, and if I had known it first, I would never have taken the job to begin with. I was sitting on the board of directors for a large mental health and substance abuse treatment center in our county. I really loved this mission and this organization. I had seen so many people and families that just fell apart during the meltdown. We had a community full of wounded people. Their scars just weren't visible. I was committed to supporting mental health and substance abuse services.

Here was my line in the sand. I was not going to quit this board. I also was not ready to give up on The Bungalow. Mentally, I began to explore leaving the Legislative office. Sitting behind the legislative desk and wearing the name badge, I no longer had a voice. Back at the white tablecloth luncheons, I was introduced as "Linda White, here representing the 'Honorable State Representative.'" The polite applause was uncomfortable for me. I wanted to represent myself. I graciously stood and smiled, as one does when they are representing others.

In my other life, I was accustomed to speaking freely with the media about what I thought. Now I weighed my words carefully, making sure they mirrored the legislator's platform. Back at the office with the white sterile walls and the nice big desk and wearing my very important and official-looking name badge, I was expected to express the talking points that had been approved by the speaker of the house or the political platform of my boss. Everyone who called our office looking for a comment was referred to my boss, the State Representative.

It was hard for me not to have an opinion. Let me rephrase that. I had plenty of opinions. It was hard for me not to voice them.

Day after day, I sat behind my very large and important-looking desk. I even had keys and a fancy security key card to swipe. Those keys did not make me happy. The red, white, and blue keys to The Bungalow made me happy.

Here, the office walls were sterile white—not like the bold colors of The Bungalow. My work life was being dictated by the Speaker of the House and my boss, the State Legislator. At home, my life was dictated by three males and a cat. I felt like I was on the outside looking in. Everyone (even the ones who didn't like me before) was nice to me now.

Strangely enough, it did not assuage me. I was living in two worlds again. It reminded me of the way things were when Mama was sick, and I didn't want to give up anything. But learning from that experience, I knew that the worlds were too far apart for both to survive.

The Bungalow was only a few miles from the legislative office. Every day at lunch, I went back to the Bungalow. It was the only place where I really felt like me. I would make a pot of coffee in the weird coffee pot that *always* dripped on the counter, no matter how carefully I poured. And then I would take off my name badge and just be me for whatever time I could. I stared at the dark yellow quote painted on our deep-teal walls that read: **"Bold ideas are easily born in nonconforming environments."**

Indeed, they are.

In the place where I had allowed everyone else to sort their life, now I had to again sort mine. It was the place where I went back and forth between resistance and surrender. I could stay with the state, have health insurance, attend white-tablecloth luncheons with polite applause, conform, and reflect the light and the thoughts of other people. I could live someone else's life and get paid for it, or I could go back to The Bungalow and tilt at windmills.

One of my friends said I shouldn't even be thinking about leaving my state job. "You hang out with powerful people, know everything that's going on in politics and the community, and have health insurance. It's a no-brainer."

Still, the walls in The Bungalow were seductive—like fifty shades of bold, real and alive with truth telling, beckoning me to find my own truth, my own work. I felt smothered when I went back to my very important office—like my skin was too tight.

I wondered if it was the way a caterpillar felt just before it became a butterfly. Or was it just the way you felt before you died? Either way, something was going on inside me.

> *Change occurs when one becomes what she is, not when she tries to become what she is not.*
> —RUTH P. FREEDMAN

Somehow, I had to try and unravel myself.

The honorable State Representative asked me to attend a municipal association dinner. The association dinner was a very important bimonthly dinner, where all the local public officials got together. It was always "big doin's" but this particular month was especially grand.

After all, the economy was terrible, and the citizens were so miserable that the elected officials deserved a nice party every now and then.

That month, the hosting city was throwing an "Island-Party"-themed dinner, complete with mango chicken and a steel drum band. The cities always took turns hosting the bimonthly social dinners. Each one tried to outdo the others. There would be a prize for the government with the most public officials in attendance.

My honorable boss wanted me to be happy, and having been a former mayor himself during the "glory days," he loved a nice party. They made him happy, so he also assumed it would make me happy. But the glory days were gone, and the citizen-funded festivities no longer made me happy. I just wasn't in a festive mood anymore. I didn't know how I was going to tell him that I didn't want to go.

Finally I got the nerve to say to him, "About the dinner, I don't think I want to go."

Surprised and with raised eyebrow, he asked, "Why not?"

"It's too hypocritical," was my dry reply. "We're cutting everything—unemployment benefits, school funding, social service programs, pension plans, and laying off workers. Not that I don't think some of that has to be done. But still, day after day, I listen to people tell their *Bottom-Side-Up* stories of foreclosures and lost jobs and medical bills, people trying to get food stamps or restart their unemployment or get health care for their children or find a job. How can I eat mango chicken on their dime? I'm not very good at this game anymore, and if all goes well, maybe I never will be. I'd rather take the money and buy medicine for some sick child."

I thought I sounded like a democrat, but my republican boss wouldn't take it that way. He was one of the most generous people I knew. And he knew the real me—the sassy one. He wouldn't like it that I didn't go, but he would understand.

He later said that I missed a really nice dinner, and that the steel drum band was amazing. I just smiled and said, "Sounds like it was a really nice event."

In the office, the political rhetoric kept the phone lines busy. The teachers were the ones that tugged at my heart strings—not the education system, but the teachers. During that legislative session, our grandson's behaviorist was laid off. She had been a savior for us and the school as we were trying to learn how to raise this special child. In my opinion, she was way more important than funding mango chicken and a steel drum band. I'm just sayin'.

One day, while the pension reform bill was working through the legislative committee, a south Florida police officer was shot and killed in the line of duty. His wife was a kindergarten teacher. The police officers went to the school to tell her. The timing seemed cruel. I called my boss to make sure he knew. I thought: *Perhaps he should go light on the rhetoric today.*

It seemed as though the fire pension plans were really the sore spot with cities and counties. But the collective union contracts had them all pot-bound, and everyone else was paying the price. It seemed as though there should have been an easier way, but the world we now live in is *Bottom Side Up,* and easy is not an option.

I reminisced back to my first job in a garment factory in Tennessee. I worked to bring in the Union. I just wanted everyone to be paid a decent wage and to be treated fairly. I still do. But sometimes now, I think the contracts are too generous, especially in these *Bottom-Side-Up* days.

A lot of regular nongovernment families go without things they want and need, like health insurance and decent wages. I'm just sayin'.

Some Things Money Can't Buy

Despite being at the epicenter of the shifting Florida state politics, I was not only sad on the inside, I was also becoming sad on the outside. My close friends noticed.

One friend said to me one day, "What's wrong with you? It seems like you lost the dinger in your bell."

That was the day I knew I had to leave. I had to find my own voice before I lost it forever. I had to get my dinger back. After the legislative session was over, I resigned to go back to The Bungalow and try it on my own again. At least I would be tilting at my own windmills. My boss thought I wanted to leave because I had been traumatized by the threats from the union. That wasn't even close.

How do you tell someone you are resigning because the office walls are white, and eating the mango chicken on a white tablecloth at the country club makes you feel like a fraud? I was lost in the woods of my own life. I saw all the parts of the whole. I did not want to be labeled a Democrat or Republican. I was a complicated person, caught in the crosswinds of being fiercely independent and still feeling a strong desire to belong, to find meaning, to make a difference. It seemed like everyone

I knew wanted to belong to some political party—everyone except me. I didn't want to be labeled or told how to think. I was at the center of my own existence, except, I didn't know what that was.

After giving proper notice, I trained my new replacement for the legislative office. She was efficient and happy. She looked nice behind the important desk.

As I was leaving on my final day, I waved at a group of protesters outside the legislative office. I thought about getting a sign and joining them. At least they had an opinion, and they weren't afraid to show it. All I knew that day was that I loved walls that were painted "fifty shades of bold" and my own voice—even if I had no words.

Hopefully, someday they would come.

I guess they have.

We are aware of our hunger and our needs, but still ignorant of what will satisfy them.
—"GIFT FROM THE SEA," ANNE MORROW LINDBERGH

After leaving the legislative office, I took a vacation by myself and tried to think about what to do next. Jerry couldn't go with me. Our grandson was still in school, and that just made me feel all the more alone. They had become like two peas in a pod. He filled the void for Jerry.

Back at The Bungalow, my business partner, too, was fading away. After all, he had to make a living for his family, and this thing that we were trying to do—engaging government and community in micro-development—was really hard. He wasn't really prepared for doing business with the government or the lies they told you anyway. I wasn't sure about anything or anybody anymore.

Mid-2011

Do you have the patience to wait until the mud settles and the water is clear?
—LAO TZU

Bottom Side Up

People called me like I was still the Chamber of Commerce. They wanted The Bungalow to be the Chamber of Commerce—just for free. They dropped off resumes and asked for maps, the kind the Chamber used to print—the one with business ads and important phone numbers and the pineapple logo.

I felt like a ghost—someone who had died but couldn't pass to the other side. I couldn't believe the community still missed the Chamber of Commerce maps, the paper ones, with the pineapple logo. Sometimes they brought an old one by The Bungalow, telling me how they needed a new one. It seemed strange, but everything in *Bottom Side Up* is strange.

So I decided to create a new map. This map could be different because I didn't have any political boundaries now. So I created a new region, including some towns in the next county. That was a map I couldn't have created at the chamber. It would have been politically incorrect. The map cover was very "Huckleberry Finnish," with two shirtless boys fishing in the St. Johns River, the one that runs north. I named it "Simple Pleasures." Lots of people were excited about it. We would sell advertising around it, just like I had done at the Chamber.

We tried to use local cartography people, but they just couldn't seem to get their arms around what we wanted.

"What do you mean you want to expand into the next county?"

"It's just lines on a map," I said. But they were used to political boundaries. See, every damn thing is about politics. We finally found a place in another state that could do the cartography and tried to use a local print company. But halfway into the project, the printing company went belly-up, and there we were again, *Bottom Side Up*.

We refunded everyone's money and shut down the project. That was really the last straw for me.

Note to self: You can't build a house during an earthquake.

I had gotten pretty good at working political campaigns, and that summer I was managing the campaign for a candidate in the local mayor's race. That would be over soon, and I was just too tired to tilt at anymore windmills. My connection to the city that I had once loved seemed to be fading. The community that once made my heart race with happiness every morning when I crossed into the city limits now just seemed like a sad and pathetic place run by bureaucrats that I didn't even know. Almost everyone had been fired by the new manager. It truly was the Alzheimer's City. I knew it, but it didn't know me. And no matter the outcome of the mayor's race, nothing would change for me. The players might change, but the stage would still be the same. I felt like a child who had been sent to bed early.

> *You only have power over people so long as you don't take everything away from them. But when you've robbed a man of everything, he's no longer in your power, he's free again.*
> —ALEKSANDR SOLZHENITSYN

The nights of September and October that year were long and sleepless. I would awaken around 3:00 a.m., tossing and turning almost every night. *What to do. Where to go. How to get out of Bottom Side Up.*

At least the "inner critic" didn't get inside my head much anymore.

The business people and others in the community asked me to try to restart the Chamber, but I knew the economy was still too weak to support much of anything. I wasn't sure chambers of commerce would even survive in the new world of social media anyway. I had to find a way to let go.

My reading had turned from business development, politics, and leadership to more spirit-quested material. After leaving the State office, I didn't have much desire to work with government again anyway, unless they were going to let me solve community problems by engaging people. I was pretty sure that wasn't going to happen anytime soon.

One night while reading, I came across an article that said, "the Hour of the Wolf" is when God answers you back. It was said that the leaders of ancient tribes would awaken at 3:00 a.m., leave their shelter, and go outside to look up at the stars and listen for inner wisdom to direct them where to move their tribe. I wondered if that was what was happening to me, except I didn't have a tribe anymore. So rather than toss and turn, I just started to get up and write. Jerry still shuffled around in his underwear to inquire, "You okay?" And by now, I had also stopped boring him with rants about unanswered prayers or wanting to move or trying to explain to him that I was lost in the woods of my own life.

I usually just smiled and said, "Yep, I'm fine."

In the wee hours of the morning, I wrote anything that came to mind, and sometimes I found a few nuggets of wisdom that made sense to me. It was during these early-morning, "hour-of-the-wolf" writings that I knew it was time to leave The Bungalow. My dreams of redevelopment and historic preservation initiatives and of working on the commuter rail project were over. I had a feeling that the commuter rail project was going to be a boondoggle anyway—a very expensive boondoggle.

No one even much talked about the project anymore. I had left the plans for the opening community celebration on my desk when the Chamber closed. The new ones that had been created by my company were gathering dust somewhere in a box.

Some songs are left unsung.

My friend Greg used to say that The Bungalow was more like a sanctuary than an office. Perhaps the universe had never wanted it to be about business. My banker friend said that I loved the community so much and all the people that were going through such hard times that I created a shelter from the storm for them. My financial manager much preferred it to be a business office, making money.

Perhaps, as Greg said, it was indeed a sanctuary where you could come to sort out your problems, to find hope, to regroup, to figure out who you are without a business card. Thinking back, The Bungalow really created itself anyway.

> *You can pour your heart out singin' a song that you believe in, and tomorrow they'll forget you ever sang.*
> —MARTINA MCBRIDE

I knew I would have to go home empty-handed and face the daunting task of renegotiating and re-storying my life. If I survived, I would have to endure the transformational pain of "coming back as something else." I would have to take raw materials and lessons learned from my time at The Bungalow and try to build a new basket to hold whatever was left of me. Damn, I was getting tired of doing this over and over and over. It really was like *Groundhog Day*.

And so with much sadness, I made the decision to close The Bungalow in December. I would stay until the election was over. On election night in November of 2011, The Bungalow, tiny and magic, was filled with the political in-crowd of three cities, anxiously awaiting election results. The media had joined us as well. As the results rolled in, some of my best friends had won their elections. Again, I found myself watching from without and within. My candidate had won a local mayor's race, unseating the incumbent mayor, and my best friend had been elected to a city council seat. My CPA had also been elected to a city council seat in the same city as my mayor friend. One would think that I would have felt on top of the world.

Everyone believed that having my friends in high places would allow me to be able work again in the community, since it was politics that had put me out of business in the first place. But I knew better. It was time to move on.

When you come to a fork in the road, take it.
—YOGI BERRA

So here was the proverbial fork in the road. They would take one fork; I would take another. They would become part of HAL's club, pot-bound by rules and regulations that bureaucrats would tell them they could not change. And they would attend the mango chicken dinners, hand the problems off to the managers, and complain about the citizens who complained about them. They would become the sun, and, if I stayed, I would become the moon, only capable of reflecting their light.

I wanted more. I wanted my own light, and I wanted to reflect the people's light. And besides, I really didn't like HAL very much anymore anyway; although, individually, I still adored each of them.

News of The Bungalow's closing broke right after the election amid rumors that I would be awarded some political job or contract by one of my best friends, who was now was in the seat of political power. No one believed I was leaving—to go nowhere. I didn't tell them the real truth.

Despite believing in individual people, especially those I had helped get into office, I had little faith in the government system to which they were entering. I believed we were experiencing what is known in medical terminology as "latent failures," where bad things happen because the entire system is in failure, and a system where individuals have little control over outcomes. For so long, the politicians had been my sun, and I had been their moon, reflecting their light—a light that I could sadly no longer see.

> *We cannot be filled unless we are first emptied, to make room for what is to come.*
> —THOMAS MERTON

I did not tell them what I knew they could not understand: that I was beginning a journey of what I later came to know as "Pratyhara." *Pratyhara* is a word frequently used in yoga practice and is the moment when we decide to let our answers come from within. I felt like a scared skydiver, standing in the door of an airplane. I had made the decision to jump. Somehow, someway, I had to find the courage to let go.

I struggled with the fact that I might be wrong about the government, and that I might be leaving The Bungalow too early. But then I saw some activity in the city park one day and discovered the city was getting ready to start showing movies in the park—bread and circuses. That's all they wanted for the people. And sadly, I believed that the citizens would settle for this. That was the day I was disappointed in the citizens too.

I wanted them to rise up, to be bold, and to ask for what they wanted. But they were tired and disillusioned too. They were going to settle for a movie in the park and free popcorn. And I was going home—for good.

I was sad.

Late 2011

Desperation is the raw material of drastic change. Only those who can leave behind everything
they have ever believed in can hope to escape.
—WILLIAM BURROUGHS

Saying Good-Bye to The Bungalow

I sorted through the proposals and the paperwork and the items at The Bungalow one by one. I donated almost everything to a charity for the homeless. The office had been set up more like a house than an office anyway. It seemed as though we were always strategizing or sharing stories over food.

I cried as I packed the boxes…again.

After having been broken open so many times, I was no longer afraid of the tears. They are just melted anger or sadness or some other pent-up emotion. Nobody was looking anyway.

My friend, the new mayor, came by to help me pack up. He said that he was sad to see me go. When I told him I was leaving, he said, "Well you can't just go."

And I said to him, "Well I can't just keep staying. It doesn't make good business sense. The manager will never support any of my projects, and she's not going to let you support any of my projects either. I won't put you in that position."

He seemed grateful—sad, but grateful.

On one of the last mornings before I was to close the The Bungalow, I came in to find everything in The Bungalow in disarray. Small flower pots overturned, papers scattered, glass objects broken. It was a mess. It was strange and I thought someone must have broken in and trashed the office. But on deeper inspection, I surmised that a bird, or perhaps several, had somehow gotten in through the fireplace chimney and messed up everything. It seemed like The Bungalow was angry that I was leaving. I was angry about leaving too. I felt like Santa Clause quitting Christmas. I still had so many gifts left in my bag.

That day, the mayor came by again and saw all the mess the birds had caused. He laughed and told me that he was going to bring me a movie that would explain it all. The next day, he brought me the movie, *Mr. Majorium's Wonder Emporium.* It was the story of a once-magic and remarkable emporium run by Mr. Majorium. As he was preparing to die, he bequeathed the emporium to a store worker. The store was so sad about Mr. Majorium leaving that it began to grieve and lose its magic. Even the walls turned gray. The Mayor said that The Bungalow was sad that I was going, and it was losing its magic.

That night at home, I watched the movie and cried, and Jerry even teared-up, watching me cry.

"I'm sorry you're having to give up the Bungalow. Everybody loves that place so much."

And even though I was sad, it was a good message for me as I closed the Bungalow. I hoped that perhaps I had brought some magic to the people who came and told their stories around my farm table. They certainly had brought magic and healing and a sense of belonging to me. The last days at The Bungalow were bittersweet. Well-wishers came by to see the magic bungalow and get a hug just one more time. They all said they wished I would stay.

It wasn't like the last day at the Chamber. At least here I got to hug people and say good-bye.

Perhaps it was the closure I had been seeking all along. I locked the door on The Bungalow for the last time and turned to face the wind. Dammitt, I had lost the keys again.

Linda S. White

The woman who cherished her suffering is dead.
I am her descendent....
I want to go on from here,
fighting the temptation to make a career of pain.
—ADRIENNNE RICH

Driving away from The Bungalow on that sunny December day was like dying all over again. I had found myself in another place of unknowing. I now realize that this is the place where true restoration begins.

PART THREE

Coming Back as Something Else

Never be afraid to fall apart because it is an opportunity to rebuild yourself the way you wish you had been all along.

—RAE SMITH

Bottom Side Up

I moped around though Christmas. It was good to have a child in the house. He kept my mind off myself and the fact that I had no parties to go to and no boxes of Christmas cards to send. During my other life, I always invited the Chamber staff to my house for our Christmas party. It was one of my favorite days of the year. I loved entertaining them. I tried to make the day special to show them how much I appreciated them. Everything was homemade, and I used my best holiday dishes—no paper plates for them.

But this year, there was nothing.

I was so lonely and empty. If someone had dropped a quarter down my throat, it would have made a clinking sound. I still missed Mama and going home to Tennessee for Christmas. I missed just about everything and everybody.

For about the hundredth time in four years, I was again begging Jerry to move.

"I want to go home" (back to Tennessee), I told him.

He just looked at me and said, "Linda, you are at home."

I didn't feel that way. I didn't feel like I belonged anywhere. I was glad for the holidays to be over, but I still had no idea what to do next. On New Year's Eve, I didn't even make any resolutions.

Our grandson was still with us, and we were beginning to think this was going to be permanent. I just didn't know if I was up to raising a difficult child, especially with the public school system in such chaos.

Mama always told me that when I didn't know what to do next to just put one foot in front of the other one and let the "winds of life" take you wherever you were supposed to go. It seemed as good a choice as any.

2012

In January 2012, I signed up for a yoga class. I was seeking a force larger than myself—a force that would propel me to wherever I needed to be, a force larger than my confusion and fear. A force that up to now was mostly undefined.

Some wise person told me that I was on a vision quest. I asked her what that was. She said that it was a rite of passage where you go into isolation either physically or mentally, and your mind becomes open to profound insights into yourself and the world. In hindsight, she was right. What I was really seeking was myself—the one without a title or a name tag or any BHAGs (big hairy-assed goals).

> *The best way out is through.*
> —ROBERT FROST

I drove to my first yoga class with my heart racing and palms sweating. I felt anxious and afraid of some unnamed fear. In my "before" life, I had cut the ribbon on this yoga studio and spa when it had opened. It was a familiar place to me, but now it seemed unfamiliar, the kind of unfamiliar one feels in *Bottom Side Up*.

Bottom Side Up

It wasn't just that I was afraid of screwing up a downward dog posture or not being able to move as gracefully as the others. I knew that this was the dark place where I would admit to myself that I couldn't go back. I couldn't fix my career or my community or the economy or my family, much less do a downward dog. It was the place where I would accept that I had experienced another early frost, like a rose caught in an ice storm. My friends were gone, my career was gone, and my family had changed.

My relationship with Spirit was messy.

I had, on occasion and under certain circumstances, tried to bargain with Him, but that hadn't worked out well, and it usually just made me mad. Bargaining was certainly not an option in this particular case, as I didn't even know what I wanted. (You can't bargain when you don't know what to ask for.)

But here on the mat, in the silence, I would have to redefine my relationship with Spirit and with my life. I would have to give up my grudges—my defiant relationship with God. I would have to accept that life is not fair. I would have to accept that new people were now running the community, and they did not give two hoots about my past accomplishments.

One of my friends (who had also lost his job) said that we were the CBU's—caring but uninvolved. I knew he missed the community as much as I did. I would have to admit that my business had failed, and then I would have to ask the universe for that unspeakable thing called help. And mostly, I was going to have to forgive a whole bunch of people, including myself.

I was going to have to accept the child and the cat and the mounded septic tank and Jerry's early retirement and the tanked stock market and the house that was worth nothing. (I was radically grateful that we had paid it off as part of our earlier plan.)

I would have to accept that there wasn't a pot of gold at the end of the rainbow. Hell, there wasn't even a rainbow that I could see.

Linda S. White

I let go of who I am so that I become what I might be.
—LAO TZU

Arriving at the Yoga studio, my instructor greeted me with a smile. She was beautiful in a deep and calming kind of way. Without fanfare, she introduced herself and showed me where the yoga props were kept. I wasn't used to this kind of humble and quiet kind of introduction. In my "before" life, everybody was loud and bubbly and either trying to sell something or get a vote.

I very much liked this kind of introduction. I was grateful that I didn't have to make cocktail talk or give a thirty-second elevator speech about who I was or try to form a relationship or wear a paper name tag that said: MY NAME IS:_Linda_____. I was just there.

And at that moment, it seemed like the safest place in the world to be. I was barefoot, wearing a T-shirt and sweat pants. It didn't seem to matter to her that I didn't have yoga clothes. I carefully chose a mat and a blanket and entered the studio, which was quiet and dimly lit. Peaceful music played softly in the background. The instructor welcomed us and "invited" us to lie down in a comfortable position and to be open to receiving.

Receiving what? I wondered. (I was relieved that we were not going to have to go around the room saying our name and where we worked and tell what we hoped to get from the class, because I didn't have the answers for either.)

The yoga instructor's voice was gentle and strong. I worried that my body was too stiff from the years of holding in tension and emotion. I lay down on the yoga mat, face up, palms open and followed the instructions.

We would begin and end with Savasana. I didn't know a lot about yoga, but I knew this pose was sometimes referred to as the corpse pose. Suddenly, I realized that I was in the right place.

I had come here to let go of my old life—to become empty. I was relieved that I had made this choice. It was a safe place to shed.

Bottom Side Up

At the center of your being, you have the answer; you know who you are and you know what you want.
—LAO TZU

In my mind, I offered what could be considered a prayer. I did not ask for help or an answer or to win the lotto or even to help me learn the downward dog. I simply whispered, "I'm here."

The tears of relief flowed unexpectedly. I quickly wiped them away, hoping that no one noticed. I was grateful for the dimly lit room (and that I wasn't wearing makeup). I always hated the superwoman sobs (the ones where the mascara is running down your face), which was probably why I had only recently let myself cry.

I was too tired to fight, broken enough to listen.

"Find your breath. "Feel the Life Force fill you as your breath rises and falls."

My hand was on my stomach, feeling the rising and falling of my breath. Their faces floated in front of me: the chamber members that had lost their businesses, the ones I had buried, the ones who had lost their homes. the ones who had lost their jobs, the elected officials that had eaten the mango chicken at the white-tablecloth dinners, the bureaucrats that had enforced all the rules that had kept us failing, the wise strong women who had stayed with me to the closing moment of the chamber, those who had let me down, those who had held me up, the ones I had let down and the ones I had lifted up, the difficult child that we would have to raise, the connection to the community that I had missed so much.

The people I blamed; the people I loved.

My sense of belonging, my identity—all replaced by the haunting question of "Why am I still here?"

The instructor asked us to place our hands on our chest and belly and to feel the rise and fall of our breath, to feel the Life Force ebb and flow through our body. Lying on the yoga mat in silence and stillness, the rhythm of my breath seemed to awaken me. For the first time in a long time, I knew that I might be broken and confused, but there was something inside me that remained—something strong and fierce and bold.

> *Female friendships that work are relationships in which women help each other belong to themselves.*
> —LOUSIE BERNIKOW, AMONG WOMEN

I went to yoga every week. I wasn't striving or struggling any more. It just seemed like I was living on an island all by myself. It seemed as though I had awakened to the incredible loneliness that I was feeling without my office or being around people. I was living in a home dominated by three males and a cat. There seemed to be hardly any traces of me left—anywhere, even in my own home.

I still wanted to call Mama. Every now and then I would pick up the phone before I remembered that she was gone. Conversations with Jerry were short-term task-oriented things like dinner and our grandson's behavior at school and the next appointment at the behavioral center:

"Pass the salt please."

"Are we out of toilet paper?"

"This place is always out of toilet paper and milk."

What else was there to talk about? Our future was unknown.

I was craving a project, friends, my femininity, intimacy. As I mentioned earlier, my best friend had been elected to a city council seat, and I knew that she would just become another elected suit. There would be no more silly girl talk or long nightly phone conversations about HAL. Now, she was "HAL." There would be no more "talk to you tomorrow." I missed her already. I knew that we had come to a fork in the road. I was raising a special child, and she was running politics. I would go to the school, and she would go to the mango chicken dinners.

She went to the gym and for spinning. I went to the studio and practiced yoga. She sweated, I breathed. She took one fork. I took another.

Lonely for female connections, I signed up for an online creativity class from a woman in Australia. Our group was a virtual community of women from all over the world. We communicated by a closed Facebook group and video conferences. This was my first peek into the power of the virtual world. These were women who were making a difference in communities all around the world. Their thinking was fresh and supportive and audacious. I was grateful that there was only one other woman from Florida in this group. I wasn't very trusting of any women in my immediate vicinity.

It was here in this virtual community that I began to open up about raising a special-needs grandchild. They were supportive. Many of them also had special-needs children. I now understand the social isolation that can come with raising special-needs children or caring for sick family members, which was why many of us leaned into the world of social media.

I'm guessing that the isolation of the farm may have been why Mama always watched soap operas. She loved *The Guiding Light* and *General Hospital.*

Many in my group were homeschooling their children. One group was building a charter school in Australia. They were involved in solving global community problems and looked at education so much differently than we did. We talked about world events and children and how important strong, compassionate, and creative women are to the world. We never talked about politics. I thought these women didn't seem as conflicted about their femininity as females in America. They were strong and compassionate women and proud of it. They fiercely loved their husbands and their children and doing bold things for their community. They made their living, mostly as compassionate and creative entrepreneurs.

They didn't seem to fear other women, and they didn't give a hoot about government. I wondered how they were able to get so much done without government interference. When I asked, it seemed like an odd question to them. One day, I asked Jerry if we could move to another country. That made him mad.

He was an Air Force veteran and, "By god, Linda," he said, "America is the best country in the world."

I wasn't too sure about that either right now. But I never brought it up again. And neither did he. I loved to hear about the lives of these other women. Money was not necessarily in their "happily ever after." Most of them had, as they said, "taken off the golden corporate handcuffs." Their freedom was more important than a big house or a Louis Vitton purse.

I came to trust them and couldn't wait for our conference calls or video conferences. After all, they didn't live here, so they couldn't hurt me. I loved hearing their stories about how they were changing the corners of the world they lived in. I didn't have much to share, but my emptiness was filled by their achievements and their laughter. I loved hearing them laugh.

Virtual was nice, but I wanted real women friends—the ones you could laugh with and drink wine with in person. I missed Mama and Sandy and Helen and Georgette and all the other women in my "before" life. I missed "see you tomorrow" and "call me later."

And then one day and I saw an advertisement in the local paper from a woman who was starting a creativity class. The class was a twelve-week class, studying *The Artist Way,* by Julia Cameron. So I called her up, properly introduced myself, and asked "Could I come to meet you before your group starts because I might want to take the class?"

Despite my loneliness, I wasn't too keen on trusting a bunch of women or anyone for that matter.

We laugh about it now, and Cheryl (who is a professional storyteller, which I think is so cool) tells the story about how I interviewed her, which is how she knew I had a "trust issue." So after the interview, I signed up for the class, where I met ten other women and learned the "Artist Way" rules of engagement. There, I found a feminine environment of support and trust. I was already familiar with these rules of engagement from the Australia Group. I though how great it would be if politics could have some Artist Rules of engagement—a supportive environment where people could engage and solve problems—right.

Never gonna happen. Well maybe somewhere—but not here.

My new group read *The Artist Way*, wrote our "Morning Pages," and met every Tuesday night for discussion.

During the discussions, I was mostly quiet. I wanted to trust them. I wanted to open my heart and tell them how much I just liked being with them on Tuesday evening and talking about life. But I just couldn't open up. I was still too wounded.

I kept thinking about how I had been betrayed so publicly by the people I thought were my friends. One night, about six weeks into the class, I started to "break open," with all my trust issues. We began to share our personal stories, and here I found what I was craving, what I had lost—a tribe of women like I had in my "before" life.

I now know there is no stronger medicine than the healing power of women when they come together and open their hearts with compassion and creativity.

Mid-2012

Trying to Let Go of the Monkey Bar

The writer Nelle Morton describes the place where one goes after the "Falling Apart": "An awful abyss that occurs after the shattering and before the new reality appears."

In the late winter of 2012, that's where I was. Despite the fact that I was going to yoga every week and also enjoying the support of the tribe, I was still lost. I was living with one foot in the political world and one foot in my emerging creative world. I was trying to learn to trust. I turned down a couple of job opportunities. The reasons were complex—even to me.

Having a special-needs child in the house left much less "me" time. I couldn't work the nights, weekends, holidays, and sixty-hour weeks that I used to; perhaps, I didn't even want to, even if we didn't have our grandson. But I was coming to accept the fact that my new family life had dramatically altered the way I could work. The school called constantly, wanting us to pick our grandson up every time he misbehaved. It was exhausting. I wondered how other working parents did it.

And the truth was, it was the reason he was living with us. His mother couldn't balance the pressure from his school and her work. I thought it was an unfortunate clash between school and parents and one that needed to get resolved.

The other reason was that I wanted to work for myself and build my own brand. I wanted to integrate all that I had learned into something new. The truth was that I didn't really want to go back to the same environment. I had changed. I wanted everybody else to change too.

Pieces of April and It's a Morning in May

I was still confused about where I belonged. I had developed a creative time-management program called Rhythmnicities™. The program integrated mind/body creative processes with day planning. The work was truly a blend of the old me with a creative twist. The program was a radical change to day and life planning, one that recognized the human need for rhythm and order, despite the chaotic frazzled world that pulled at us every moment of every day.

I finally got the nerve to share the program with the tribe. They spent a half day listening to me rattle on and talk about every aspect of the program. Over wine and lunch, they critiqued in the most loving way. They encouraged me to share it with others. I began doing focus groups wherever I could find a few women with a couple of hours. Despite the fact that almost everyone who took the workshop loved it, I did not know how to integrate the program into a paid workshop program or how to claim my new found creativity. But at least I was moving toward something.

Bottom Side Up

Back in the community, the political landscape was heated and full of political hopefuls. This was a presidential election year, so everyone was more ginned up than usual. Our entire lives seemed to be consumed by one long endless campaign commercial. I was grateful for the creative and nurturing interruption of the tribe. It seemed as though national and local politics consumed every aspect of our lives. It reminded me of a Toby Keith song, "I Love this Bar."

Politicians dressed in suits and sweating like pigs in the summer heat claimed their love and support for veterans, while the suicide numbers and homelessness among veterans continued to rise. Women politicians hit the campaign trail soliciting the female vote, while turning their backs in their own communities to local females struggling to stay in business. I knew all too well; I had been one of those women.

No matter how many times I vowed to stay out of politics, they called to me like a siren. The truth was that I was pretty good at the game, and maybe I enjoyed it more that I cared to admit. Early in the spring, I had the opportunity to work on the incumbent sheriff's campaign team. I had known him for years and knew him to be a good man and a good sheriff. There wouldn't be any surprises in his campaign. He is a "what-you-see-is-what-you-get" kind of person.

The office was nonpartisan in our county, but the Sheriff was a republican and his opponent a democrat. It was the first time that we had seen the partisan politics play out so openly in local nonpartisan elections.

The Sheriff was determined to keep the campaign unpolarized and nonpartisan, despite the partisan vortex swirling around us. Committed to maintaining respect and trust, even with those who opposed him, he was wise enough to know that he would need the support of the entire community after the campaigns were over. He understood clearly the empowering ability of the people and of owning your own power.

Despite the Sheriff being a registered republican, our campaign embraced both parties. He ran without getting sucked into any of the political camps. Somehow, he managed to maintain the support of both the republicans and democrats. The campaign was actually a respite and a shelter from the storm of all the nasty partisan politics and polarizations that were swirling around us. Working in his campaign helped me stay out of all the other campaigns that were pressing me for involvement, even some that I personally and quietly supported. The Sheriff was a man who had control of helicopters, swat teams, guns, and tanks. In fact, he had access to a small army. Yet, he was always patient and fierce in his belief of reaching across the table to those who disagreed with him. He favored building consensus over creating conflict and frequently reminded his campaign team, "Remember that this is an election, not a war."

The Sheriff never knew it (unless he reads this book), but the campaign and watching him work across party lines and political opposition were causing huge shifts in the way I viewed politics. The election was a landslide in his favor, despite a very strong democratic vote. It proved that voters will cross party lines for leaders who inspire trust and confidence. It is that which we crave.

In this laboratory of politics, something else started to emerge in me. My thoughts were beginning to crystalize. I very clearly knew the ideals, the values, and the people I believed in and why. My ideals were neither democrat nor republican, but the best parts of both. They were the conservative and strong work ethic from my farm life combined with compassion and empowerment. The people I believed in loved community over politics. I was now able to see the traits of the most effective political leadership, and it had nothing to do (at least in my mind) with their party affiliation.

I had developed some very good friendships within the local Republican party. They seemed to like me, but I wondered if they would still like me if I weren't a republican. And then I thought back to the Partnership Project. The ones who destroyed that project were mostly democrats, and back then, I was one of them (well not really, but I was a registered democrat).

So I made a mental note not to let that stand in the way of redefining my political ideology.

Bottom Side Up

Angels and Elected Officials

In the same city where The Bungalow was located (the place I always loved), three schools (elementary, middle, and high) had been constructed during the boom years. But as the economy tanked, the school system also encountered financial difficulty. Our school board policy dictated that bus services would not be provided for children within a two-mile radius of the school. In this particular case, a busy major state highway runs through the heart of the area. This caused children to have to walk cross this state highway, sometimes in the early morning hours before daylight. The half-mile corridor leading from the state highway to the school (believe it or not) had no streetlights and only partial sidewalks. Several children had been hit by cars during the previous year.

The bureaucrats had studied the problem to death, and still nothing had been done, except reminding everyone to be careful. And then one morning, crossing the highway before daylight, a young boy on his way to school was tragically struck and killed.

I had managed the new mayor's campaign, and I knew him to be a man of compassion. As a father of five, he was haunted by the untimely death of this child. It had happened in his city, and he took the tragedy personally. It was the kind of deep soul pain that I knew was powerful enough to move beyond bureaucratic power of government managers or a school board or state transportation bureaucrats.

Having lost a child myself, I understood more than most the deep soul pain of these tragedies. The mayor and I talked about how to resolve the issue. We physically traced the journey that the children took each morning to see what they saw. We drove it at first, but that didn't get me close enough. I wanted to experience what the children were actually experiencing.

So one morning, I got up at 5:30 a.m. and walked the road to the school in the dark. Actually seeing what the children saw opened my eyes and my heart. I couldn't understand why we would build schools, force children to walk there, and then not install streetlights or create crosswalks for a busy state highway.

So while the female city manager was out of town, the Mayor and I and one of the leaders of a local community organization hatched up a plan. The community organization fronted the money to lease a couple of event tower lights and we positioned them at the crosswalks. The neighbors let us set up a generator on their property. We set up the lights the night before and had everything ready for the following morning. I wanted to be there when they turned the lights on. I wanted to see the children's faces.

Excited that morning, I called the mayor at 5:30 a.m., "Get up, Mayor, and come on down to the school crossing. We're going to poke a hole in the universe this morning." (That's what I say before we do something pretty bold.)

And we did.

Just as the children started their morning walk, the mayor and the community leader cranked up the generator and happily shouted, "Let there be light." It was an amazing thing to behold. The kids smiled and waved as they crossed the newly lit streets.

"Thank you for the lights," they yelled.

The Mayor and the community leader waved back, "You're welcome."

That particular community leader had just successfully emerged from a battle with acute leukemia, so he wasn't afraid of breaking the rules either. I watched with proud and tear-filled eyes. Of course, I had arranged for media coverage, and they were able to tell the story of how the mayor and a community organization had lit up the street for the children. I knew the street to the school would never be dark again. Once you've seen the light, you can never be satisfied going back into the darkness.

Later that day, the Sheriff called, and I told him the story about the lights. He also wanted to help and sent his traffic division to study and redesign the traffic patterns. The Mayor vowed to turn the lights on every morning for as long as it took to get the streetlights installed. And then the strangest thing happened. The District Congressman, the same one who called me right after 9-11, convened a transportation workshop to create a sense of urgency with the bureaucrats to install streetlights and crosswalks. And the State Legislator, the one I had worked for, along with the Sheriff and the Mayor, all got together and fixed that terrible problem. Some said it was just political season.

But I know these men, and I think it was the pain of one mayor in a small city who said, "The children in my city deserve better than this," and a community leader with the creativity and courage to put up temporary lights while the manager was out of town. Together, they made an entry point for other strong leaders to help solve a problem. It was pretty easy once the problem got moved from bureaucrats to elected leaders. And just as I predicted, the road to the schools was never dark again. The state road now has traffic lights at the crosswalks, and the traffic flows in a much more safe and orderly fashion. They all worked to tame the chaos rather than accept it.

The Mayor smiled and told me later, "Linda, you told me that morning that we were going to poke a hole in the universe, and indeed, we did."

Smiling from ear to ear, I replied, "I hope we poke so many holes in the universe it starts to look like swiss cheese."

My only haunting question in that entire story was, "Where were the women?" It wasn't that we didn't have any women in leadership positions. It just seemed that they were missing in action on this particular issue—the one where children were being injured and losing their lives. I'm just sayin'.

Blackberry Summer
2012

As spring turned into summer, I was working on the Sheriff's campaign, teaching a creativity workshop every now and then, and still trying to figure out where I belonged. To tell the truth, I was hiding in plain sight.

Late that summer, I cut some stalks of an accumulation of withering herbs from my herb garden, the same garden that grew the bundle of rosemary that I sent with Mama on her angel flight back home. I bundled them up to dry and hung them *Bottom Side Up* in my Florida Room.

By the way, I remind you again that this is the room where I write, rant, pray, and watch the moon come up over the lake, and sometimes, it's where we sit and stare at the lake when something is "bad wrong."

I didn't know how long it would take for the herbs to dry, and I had no idea why they were supposed to be hung *Bottom Side Up* when drying. I just did what the instructions said. (Occasionally, I still follow directions.) And then one morning, I got up, poured my coffee, and went to the Florida room to sit in my oak swing and ponder my shifting life. When I pulled back the sliding glass doors, the Florida room was filled with at least a hundred beautiful monarch butterflies. The scene was absolutely surreal. My eyes welled up with unexpected tears, and I called for Jerry to come quick: "You gotta see this."

He could sense the urgency in my voice and quickly headed in my direction, asking me what was wrong. When he entered the Florida room and saw the butterflies, he too was awestruck.

"Where did they come from?"

And then we noticed the dried herbs hanging *Bottom Side Up*, and upon close inspection, we could see the empty cocoon shells still attached to the stalks. Still crying, I opened the door and, without a moment's hesitation, the butterflies took flight. Their new wet wings gracefully lifted them toward the sky. They were so beautiful. I wanted to keep them, but I knew they would die if I tried to hold on to them too long. Perhaps yoga had taught me the art of letting go. They had been hanging *Bottom Side Up* in a small dark place for the longest time. But that day, their cocoon "broke open and fell apart." Sure enough, they "came back as something else"—something really spectacular. It was the damnedest and most sacred metamorphosis I had ever seen.

And that was the day I knew for sure I wouldn't always be *Bottom Side Up*.

Without struggling or tilting at windmills to trying to save the world, I spent the rest of that year writing, working at the edges of politics, hanging out with my tribe of women friends, practicing yoga, and trying to un-remember all the things that were keeping me pot-bound. I was trying to let go of the monkey bar.

The tribe and yoga were sparking my creativity, and the Sheriff's campaign was shifting my political ideology.

That summer, I was lucky enough to get into a teleconference writing class from SARK, Susan Kennedy, who is an American author and illustrator of self-help books. Five of her fifteen books have been best sellers. I considered myself lucky to be in her class. We had hour-long discussions with SARK every Thursday night.

She named me "Deep Diver" and pushed me to write until I could finally write an article that could actually stir her soul. It was very difficult for me to write from my soul. I was used to writing business or political articles, but soul-writing is different. It was forcing me to explore that which I most feared—showing my vulnerability. I finally wrote an essay called, "Seasons of Her Grief."

It was the story of a woman who, for years, had put flowers on the roadside at the place where her child had died one rainy night while trying to cross a busy road. Right after that essay and during a critique of my writing, I asked SARK what else I needed to work on.

She said to me, "Linda, you don't need to do anything else except write—just write from your soul and put it out into the world. Your stories are medicine for the world. And so I began to write this book. Or perhaps it began to write itself. Much of it I had already written in bits and pieces as I tried to make sense of my fragmented life. I only needed to sew it together. It was SARK who taught me to claim my own stories.

The tribe was wicked good for me. We laughed and cried, drank wine, made art, showed up sometimes with no makeup, and confessed to occasionally eating cookie dough or ice cream from the box. We talked about almost everything: religion, sex, art, and creativity. We rarely ever talked about politics, and that was good for me. They taught me how to play and laugh again. That farm girl in me worked way too much and took life too seriously. But mostly, they taught me to trust again. I just needed (as we all do) a good bunch of friends and a safe place to land and perhaps a willingness to get bruised up if I lived passionately.

Yoga was also causing huge shifts in me. I was becoming much less attached to the thought that I needed a name tag. While my head was seeking a consistent source of income with a name tag, my heart was listening from within. Thankfully, my heart spoke the loudest. But I still faced hard decisions.

My COBRA insurance from the state was running out. I finally decided that I would continue working for myself. So I began the daunting task of finding health insurance on my own. The process was frightening—so frightening that I thought about just trying to find a *J-O-B*, any job that might provide benefits. I could now understand why people stay in jobs they hate just for health insurance. My current insurance plan offered a conversion which was terribly expensive, and then there was another plan I could apply for. I called it the "perfect plan." It was considerably less expensive. The catch was that you had to be nearly perfect: good credit, no traffic violations, weight within normal limits, lab work perfect, and blood pressure perfect.

My new life was much less stressful, and I was eating well and doing yoga. I was feeling better than I had in years, so I applied for the "Perfect Plan." A paramedical came to my house, weighed me, and took all my personal information. Then she took a couple of vials of blood, and I peed in a cup. She took all my "stuff" and drove off into the sunset. I would get insurance if everything was perfect.

Several days later, the agency, which was subcontracted from my insurance provider, called and said that they needed to repeat my lab work. I immediately suspected that something was wrong with me. Anxiously, I demanded an explanation. They sheepishly informed me that the paramedical who had taken my personal information and my personal body fluids had not turned them in, and they weren't really sure where she was. They thought she had been hospitalized, and that she was coming home soon, and that all my "stuff "was at her house.

The story was just too confusing for me to understand. What the hell? Had she stolen my identity? Did she sell my body fluids? Should I shut down my bank account? What did I need to do? I felt angry and violated and scared. Somehow, they miraculously recovered all my stuff from her house, and, as it turned out, I got the perfect insurance.

That was my first awakening on what the future of health insurance might look like. I didn't much like what I saw. What if I had been sick or had gained too much weight or had high blood pressure? It is a harsh reality for Americans, and especially for those of us who are *Bottom Side Up*, health matters!

Since I was re-storying my whole life and probably wasn't ever going to get to work on a community project again, I pondered which way to go next. I thought about reactivating my physical therapy license. I had put it on inactive status almost ten years ago, thinking I would run the chamber of commerce until I retired. I would need to take more than one hundred hours of continuing education. The thought seemed overwhelming.

I studied online, trying to recall the names of bones and nerves and muscles. My stomach would knot up when I thought about going through all of the immunizations and tests and rules and documentation. I would not be healing people. I would just be filling out forms and checking boxes and trying to make sure that I didn't violate any of the pages and pages of policies and procedures.

And then I remembered why I left the health-care field in the first place. But what did light me up was exploring ways to become healthier. I thought more about wellness than I did sickness, especially because of my illness before the chamber closed. I now know that was brought on by stress.

Why couldn't we as communities talk more about wellness and health? Jerry had been diagnosed with type 2 diabetes. He was taking medicine for high blood pressure and cholesterol and diabetes. Every medicine had a side effect. I though how much healthier he could be if he just did some basics, ate better with smaller portions, and exercised. But that was just me thinking out loud.

I quit taking the continuing education classes. I simply was not hungry enough to go back there to that sick place yet. Total knee replacements just didn't excite me. Most of the tribe women were pretty healthy. They did things like positive affirmations, and they focused on wellness and nutrition, although they were not above occasionally eating ice cream from the box either. That's what I loved about them. They really amazed me. They made it look so easy and never talked about being sick. One of them even owned a franchise for a health magazine. (Keep reading to see what surprises life had in store for me in early 2013.)

> *I didn't see it then, but it turned out that getting fired from Apple was the best thing that could have ever happened to me. The success of being successful was replaced by the lightness of being a beginner again, less sure about everything. It freed me to enter one of the most creative periods of my life.*
> —STEVE JOBS

The days turned into weeks and then into months. Night after night I would sit in in the Florida Room, looking out over the lake. I watched the rising and the setting of the sun and the moon each taking turns, dancing in a spiral rhythm.

Rising and setting. Waxing and waning. Light and shadow.

I watched from without and within, trying to own the rhythms of my own life.

Sometimes I would sit in my handmade oak swing, curled up in a question-mark ball, pondering my life, remembering my childhood on the farm, and wondering if life was just passing me by. Still, I was holding out for "something more." There had to be more to this thing called life. There had to be more to being a human than just existing and running through life like a hamster on a wheel.

Bottom Side Up

I would not settle for anything less—just yet. I grew especially fascinated by the moon. At times it would be too dark to see. The next night, a tiny sliver of light would begin to emerge from the darkness. And then a few days later, almost as if by magic, just as nightfall came, the most beautiful full round moon would rise into the night sky, lighting up everything around it.

Its reflection into the lake caused the water to look as though it was a field of sparkling diamonds.

And just at the time it was breathtakingly beautiful, it would begin its waning journey back into total darkness. The predictable rhythm became comforting to me. No matter what chaos was occurring in the world, no matter how confused or sad I was, the stock market could be up or down, I could be sick or well, it didn't matter. The rhythm of the moon was unchanged. The moon kept moving in the rhythm of light and darkness, seeming to love each phase the same.

In my question-mark ball, I pondered how it could love the dark as much as the light. Then one night, I realized that the moon knows that its darkness will turn into light, just as it knows that its light will also turn back to darkness. The heart knows its beat will be followed by rest, and the ocean knows its tide will come in and go out.

If only I could find such faith.

Late in the summer, Kim, one of the women in the tribe who was really a great photographer, got the creative courage to do a photo exhibit of us. The exhibit was called the "Transformation Tribe." She portrayed each of us in the artful and creative ways that we each were dealing with the struggles of our changing lives. She photographed me at the edge of my backyard lake, kneeling down, looking up to the moon, searching for the "meaning of life." I had butterfly wings on my back. I thought she captured the essence of where I was in life.

Much to our surprise, the photo exhibit was a big hit in the community. All of us were nervous about allowing the public to see the deeper and more fragile side of our life. It felt very vulnerable. I had been photographed publicly hundreds of times, but I had always been wearing my business suit, and I had always known the answer. This time, I was photographed as an uncertain woman with butterfly wings coming out her back. Did I mention that *Bottom Side Up* can make people do strange things?

The local newspaper featured us in a story, and a regional TV station featured us in the "Making a Difference" section. During the newspaper interview, the reporter asked me what it felt like when I found myself in the wall after the Chamber closed.

The question felt like a knife searing through my gut. It was the first time I had shared any of my personal reflections about the closing of the Chamber and the very sudden and public "end of an era" of my life. But it was indeed part of the breaking-open process, and so I talked about it openly and honestly. Even the reporter had tears in her eyes as I spoke. She had interviewed me many times in my "before" life, so she knew how difficult the transition had been for me.

All of the women in the tribe had transformed in some way, each of us awakening together to the courage and creativity that can be found when we come together in supportive ways. In the small acts of nurturing and tending the small creative spark in each other, our own lives had been transformed. We weren't even trying.

By now, all of us were working on some creative project. I was writing and working on Rhythmnicities™. And we all received another transformational gift. We began to be able to see through the dark. We could see transformational opportunities in the darkest of places. I guess that's the beauty of art. Artists see healing in the face of pain and beauty in the ugliest of places. They can take a simple raindrop and make it magical.

One night we were having dinner together, and I remarked that we needed a place where we could encourage and support other women in their creativity. We spotted an empty building in the downtown area. Kim, in an outlandish act of courage, leased the space, and we all voted on a creative name for the store: "Funky Trunk Treasurers."

The walls of the Funky Trunk Treasurers are painted fifty shades of bold, so the place is very happy. Kim transformed the empty building into an art consignment shop with some classroom space. We rented space from her to teach our classes. I taught Rhythmnicities™.

That fourth of July, I decided not to go to the fireworks show provided to me by the government. I put up my own flags and decorated my porch with red, white, and blue bunting. That night, I sat on my front porch, drinking homemade lemonade and eating fresh homemade blackberry cobbler, a la mode, one of Mama's favorite recipes.

The summer night sky dazzled me with the most spectacular lightning show imaginable. I still wanted to move somewhere else, but that night, I was willing to ponder if Jerry was right when he suggested, "Linda you are at home."

And then I did something totally out of character for me. I winked at God. And I kinda think that He or She winked back.

HIDING IN PLAIN VIEW

By the autumn of 2012, I had been hiding in plain view for almost three years. I came out occasionally to attend some community or political event. I stayed connected by Facebook and made a few strategic calls. Most people just assumed that I was doing something important. No one, not even Jerry, knew the depth of my transformation. I didn't talk about myself much anyway. Remember: I'm a good listener.

I had been months and months *Bottom Side Up* inside the cocoon, and while from the outside, I might have appeared contented and unchanged, inside, I was feverishly renegotiating life. I was letting my old life break open and fall apart, risking everything to follow my own wisdom and come back as "something else," not defined by a political party or an ordained religion or a membership program.

And for the first time in a long time I was moving slightly upward toward the light: the light of the sheriff's decent political campaign, the love and support of a tribe of women, and the wisdom of my yoga instructor. "The harder a thing is, the more it requires my softness."

Linda S. White

"Forgiveness is the fragrance that the violet sheds on the heel that has crushed it."
—MARK TWAIN

I had watched many, many moons come and go over the lake when the day finally came. It was a hotter-than-usual, humid Florida day in September. The local political campaign camps were fast and frenzied. Sign wavers dotted every corner. Dressed in cool, comfortable yoga clothes, I was driving to yoga class, thinking about how agonizing it must be to stand on the side of a hot Florida road, sweating profusely, dodging traffic, and waving a stupid sign trying to get a vote. I know it's all part of the political circus, but still....

And then I saw my political ex-BFF there on the side of the road, waving her sign, "driving the vote," as they say. And as I mentioned, one thing about her: she knew how to "drive the vote." She was no doubt a savvy political machine. I wondered if someone else had been elected, if my life would have been different. In the yoga studio, stretched out on the mat, I continued to reflect about us.

There she was on the hot brutal roadside, waving a sign. Here I was, relaxing on a yoga mat; she, flanked by her political tribe yelling and waving signs at honking motorists. Me, bowing my head toward my fellow yogi's, "*Namaste* (May my light meet your light)." And in that moment, forgiveness washed over me, melting the anger and the grudges that I had felt for so long.

I fell awake, knowing that, after all, she did not affect my actions without my permission, nor did I affect hers. We were once two spirals spinning in the same universe, having come together with an incredible amount of energy. Within those moments, we had made each other and our communities better. We had made the community better for women and children. And finally in my mind, I let go of the anger and resentment and sadness at what might have been. My gift to the community had been love. Her gift was political power.

Bottom Side Up

Together we made a great team. Ask me which is the most powerful. I would tell you that the real power is when the alchemy of both comes together.

I felt lucky to have been part of that for a while, to have enjoyed her rich and wicked sense of humor, her friendship, and her love of public service. Perhaps one day we could renegotiate our relationship—perhaps not.

At any rate, I was no longer angry, and that could only be good for me. I had finally stopped fighting the ghosts of my "before" life. And that day life seemed to shift for me.

In late October, I learned that an AmeriCorp Vista position was opening in our county through the National Homeless Coalition. It was strange, but I instinctively knew it was the next right thing for me. Without hesitation, I applied and was accepted for tour of duty.

In the November election, the sheriff won by a landslide vote, and another of my friends won a seat for the Florida House of Representatives. My political ex-BFF, as expected, was returned to the county commission.

The next week after the election, I packed a small suitcase and left for Atlanta to begin my training for AmeriCorp. Where I was going, I didn't need much. There would be no awards banquet at the end of this training. There would only be an oath of office ceremony, and then we would all be sent out into the world to fight poverty in some of the most difficult places.

I found it ironic that I would end up in my own county. It seemed as though I had come full circle.

For four years, I had watched the complete meltdown of the economy in our community. I had painfully watched as businesses and families lost their jobs and then their homes. Perhaps the time had come to count our losses and begin the long and painful journey forward. Hope is a strategy.

Linda S. White

The Circle of Life

In my new life, the job would be strange. Instead of trying to create new jobs, I would be trying to identify the very basics: food and shelter. Immediately, I could see that only the communities and governments that could work together would be able to restore their people and rebuild their communities. And by the way, restoring is not the same as enabling.

Restoration is a retool for self-sufficiency. Along with self-sufficiency comes empowerment and personal responsibility. As I would later learn, the balance would be a difficult one.

I was assigned as a "Partnership and Capacity Builder" for the National Homeless Coalition in the Bringing America Home project. The training was outstanding, and I chose the "Poverty in America and Building Organizational Capacity" learning track.

My first assignment was to identify and interview every food pantry in our region. My findings were astounding. Even though we were beginning to create a few jobs again, many were part-time and low-wage in Florida, where the tourism industry is king. The middle class seemed to be struggling the most. Engineering and high-tech jobs were still few and far between. The pay was half of what it used to be.

Sometimes a little extra food assistance meant that a family would be able to pay rent for another month. The other thing I noted was that much of the food at the pantries was high fat and perishable items, which was not a bad thing if you're hungry. But I thought we could do better.

Self-determining people also meant healthy people. I thought Florida, with a large agriculture industry, ought to be able to get more fresh fruits and vegetables out into the community.

And while we were re-storying our communities, I thought we ought to be creating an environment that encouraged healthier people. That Christmas, on behalf of a community foundation, I presented a check to fund a "Snack Pak for Kids" program that provided food for the weekend, when children are not able to participate in the school lunch and breakfast program.

One night, while watching TV, I heard some political person make the remark that schools should not be feeding children breakfast at all. I was livid. In the middle of the "Great Recession," he didn't want to feed children breakfast. We already had them walking to school in the dark, and he wanted to stop giving "them" breakfast—*them* being America's future. Really?

And then I started to wonder why people marched and screamed so loudly about abortion but were so quiet about children who were starved and abused and murdered after they were born. Isn't that a travesty too? America has an awful lot of rethinking to do.

Huge amounts of public dollars are being spent on economic development, while social services are being cut drastically. Mental health and substance-abuse issues are contributing heavily to homelessness and hunger, especially in children. We must find a way for the education system to wrap around the needs of these children and their families.

Floridians had retrenched after the meltdown in a not-so-good way. We had become one of the leading states in opiate pill mills, and our county was seeing a rise in drug-related deaths.

Our county also had one of the highest suicide rates in the nation, but we weren't talking about that either.

The sale of prescription pain pills had become the new economy for some doctors and dealers. It was kind of like a pyramid scheme: pay the doctor to write the prescription, buy sixty pills, sell thirty and keep thirty for yourself. The epidemic easily went viral. The high unemployment and widespread depression made it seductive. It seemed as though almost every family was being touched by either friends or family addicted to pills. This fresh hell that families were enduring had spilled over into the political landscape. The pressure to regulate pill mills was intense.

Finally, the state passed legislation to shut down pills mills. It was proclaimed as a bold step in the war on drugs, but the unintended consequence was that the addicts were out on the street without their drugs, and the drugs were harder to get, causing the price to rise. Children and families were caught in the crosshairs of a drug-addicted society. With funding cuts for mental health and substance-abuse services, there seemed little that anyone could do except watch the carnage.

At least I could try to get a weekend "Snack Pak" to hungry children. And by the way, that night after I presented the check for the Snack Pak program to the children, I reflected back on the man who had walked into the chamber when all of this started back in 2007, the man with the "Bible verse and the lotto ticket."

On my way home, I whispered a prayer for the children and stopped by the convenience store. I smiled at the guy behind the counter, "I'd like a quick-pick lotto ticket, please."

"Just one?" he asked.

"Yes, that's how you buy lotto tickets if you believe in magic."

2013

*Life is like a box of chocolate;
you never know what you're going to get.*

—FOREST GUMP

From Board Room to Homeless Camp

The irony of my life and a reminder of how far off the beaten path I had come showed up in the form of a front-page local news story in January 2013. It was a half-page story with a media photo of the Economic Partners Breakfast. The smiling face of one of my chamber chief friends was front and center. The "suits" were all seated at the white tablecloth, silver-buffet breakfast feast. The business development manager, who didn't follow through with his agreement to lease space in my chamber building, could still be seen smiling in the background.

As it turned out, he was indeed the smart one. He survived, and I didn't, but then, he was backed by government funds, and I was backed by the private sector—things that make you go hmm....

That same day, my journey took me to homeless encampments tucked away quietly in wooded areas, just barely out of site from the bustle of a city street and in the shadow of a hospital. I was participating in the National Point in Time count of homeless people.

While my former friends (i.e., "suits") were drinking coffee from shiny cups and talking about job creation at the country club, I was tromping through the woods in search of the homeless encampments.

Walking through the woods that morning, my memories and my senses turned *Bottom Side Up*. I could remember the sights and sounds and smells of the breakfasts with the "suits": the Lacoste cologne smell of the suits, the popping of the stilettos as the "ladies" walked across the Italian-tiled floors of the country clubs, the sparkling crystal glasses of water being filled from the a silver pitcher, where condensation occasionally dripped onto the white tablecloth. Here in the woods, there was only quiet, except for the occasional chirping of a bird, singing for no other reason except because it can.

The smell of sweat and spoiled food permeated the air in the empty encampments. A dirty plastic bucket with a half-used packet of epsom salts, which I supposed was medicine for a leg or foot injury, lay beside a tree stump. A handmade sign that said, "Hungry, will work for food," and a small pile of oranges splattered the tattered landscape.

After all, it was January in Florida, where oranges are abundant.

I was hot and smelled of sweat myself, having stomped through the woods for hours in search of homeless people. The count was important for funding. I was wearing boots and blue jeans and carried a few fast-food gift cards that would be distributed to homeless people who might answer my seven-page homeless-coalition-prepared questionnaire. I had already made my mind up that I would give away the gift cards even if they didn't answer my questions. I probably wouldn't have answered me either.

At home that night, I was radically grateful for a good meal on a nice plate and a hot shower with a loofa sponge filled with good-smelling bath gel. Exhausted, I snuggled down in bed under my soft clean sheets and whispered to the universe, "Thank you for everything!" And drifting off in a peaceful sleep, I reflected on the daily farm prayers of my family:

"Thank you for the food we are about to receive; thank you for the many blessings that have been bestowed upon us; thank you for the health and love of this family; thank you for another day on this beautiful place called Earth. We pray that you will give us a good night's sleep so that we may rise in the morning and do your work."

Radical gratitude was in my genes. People thought I had good manners because I said "thank you" a lot. I wasn't being polite. I was being grateful. Mama raised me that way.

Heroes or Angels (you choose what to believe) are Everywhere

And it was as if suddenly my world had become filled with the most extraordinary people. In another twist of ironic fate, one of my banker friends who had managed a foreclosure division in his "before" life was now working for Habitat for Humanity. He didn't even really know how he ended up there anymore than I knew how I ended in up in AmeriCorp. It was like finding an old friend in a foreign country. We talked for hours on end about the banking industry, the housing market, and politics. We also talked about something that was new to both of us: homelessness and the new poverty of middle class America.

We sat on the same board for a mental health and substance-abuse center and, despite looking into the abyss of broken lives, we always found something to laugh about during our conversations. Sometimes I brought graham crackers to the meetings. He called me "Groceries."

I also met an amazing man from Alabama who had lost everything he had (his business and his home) in hurricane Katrina, and yet, he was working to rebuild his community along with his own life.

By happenstance, I met a judge who was working on a jail-diversion homeless shelter. I did some work with her on the project, and we instantly became friends. She was not only smart and audaciously bold and my friend, but she restored my faith in the justice system. We talked about everything from cooking Sunday dinner to how the court system worked. I learned a lot from her. One day I asked her, "How do you make decisions in such a crazy world where everyone is lying to you and spinning the truth?"

She wisely advised, "Just go back to what you know to be true. And then you'll see the next right step."

It has turned out to be such a simple truth for me.

And then, right in the middle of all this new life, I got a brochure in the mail. It was an opportunity for licensed health-care professionals to become Certified Wellness Coaches.

They only had to invite me once. This was what I had been waiting for. So I took the class and passed the test and got my certification and then started working on the backlog of CEUs. The new track was about wellness, the mind–body connection, and stress reduction.

It was as though my previously dulled mind had become a sponge, soaking up every new piece of information I could find. I trained as a "Mental Health First Responder" and a "Field Surveillance Investigator" for outbreaks and pandemics. I studied PTSD and diabetic management and lifestyle illnesses (the ones that we can do something about). I trained to coach people to take personal responsibility for their own health.

Through AmeriCorp, I was learning how to engage large and small groups to identify and solve community problems. I was helping to feed hungry children and working on homeless prevention programs and preparing for my second wind in health, wellness, and creativity programs.

But mostly, I was on fire again—on fire with possibilities and hope.

I thought that the new personal wellness plans, along with coaching, might be a better plan than the government (HAL) regulating the size of sodas.

From the big picture, we are all broken open—broken open by acts of terrorism, school shootings, foreclosures, and fear about our future. Interesting 2013 survey data from the Associated Press reveals that four out of five Americans report that they have struggled with joblessness and near poverty for at least parts of their lives. Over the course of the last few years, we have lost our homes and our identities, and most of us have at least occasionally lost our way.

We all know what it means to be *Bottom Side Up*.

Many of us feel betrayed by our government, our health-care system, our education system, our religion, and even our own friends and family. We feel that they let us down when we need them most. Perhaps we're justified in feeling that way.

In July 2013, the popular Pope Francis, in his simple and humble message of love and understanding, offered a breathtakingly blunt explanation of why so many had turned away from their church. His same explanation can be applied to other touchstone organizations and government:

> "Perhaps the church appeared too weak, perhaps too distant from their needs, perhaps too poor to respond to their concerns, perhaps too cold, perhaps too caught up with itself, perhaps a prisoner of its own rigid formulas. Perhaps the world has made the church a relic of the past, unfit for new questions. Perhaps the church could speak to infancy but not to those who come of age. We need a church capable of rediscovering the maternal womb of mercy. Without mercy, we have little chance nowadays of becoming part of a world of wounded persons in need of understanding, forgiveness, and love."

Preach on, Pope Francis. You obviously understand *Bottom Side Up*!

Governments, education systems, health-care systems, corporate America, and nonprofits could take some lessons from the words of the Pope.

I personally see and feel our incredible despair and sense of helplessness when I hear another tragic story of a mother who killed her own children or a father who killed his family or a senior citizen who killed the spouse they loved because they couldn't see another way. I feel pain when I see homeless families living in cars or cheap motel rooms, especially in, of all places, the shadow of the Big Mouse.

Linda S. White

My heart breaks for families who have lost their children to drugs or suicide. And I am deeply saddened for diabetics that cannot afford insulin or a cashier working for minimum wage that cannot afford a dentist.

> *"My dream is of a place where America will once again be seen as the last best hope on earth."*
> —ABRAHAM LINCOLN

Each morning as my grandson gets on the bus, I offer up a wish for him and every other child: "May the system be kind to them, and may they all be safe today."

Troubled as we are, I found in my own life that breaking open and falling apart gifts us with incredible opportunities to re-story our personal lives, our families, our culture, and our nation. We *can* come back as something else. We are America, and we have a chance to do better.

We can create decent jobs in America. We have done it before. We can rebuild infrastructure and restore the inner structure of American families. None of us can do it all, but each of us can do something. Elected leaders must begin to choose empowerment over oppression. They must do what is right for America and the people they govern—not special interest groups or partisan politics. They must learn to allow people the opportunities to adapt, to grow, and to create a new kind of America.

I believe in a world that is formed but not yet emerged. It is patiently waiting for us to get our second wind and birth it in to being. And how do I know we have the resilience to do it?

Because I know people who are either heroes or angels (you choose). Most of them are not the ones on the nightly news or the front page of the local newspaper. They are the people who quietly make the world a better place. Many of them are sitting on the sidelines, and we need to get them back in the game—not as placeholders or "has beens" but as leaders.

Bottom Side Up

They are people like me who are asking the hard questions of themselves and others—the ones who are quietly waiting to get their fierce second wind and get back in the game. They are seeking to create solutions to our problems through compassion, creativity, and evidence-based outcomes.

While I was writing this book, a tragic shooting occurred in a movie theatre in Aurora, Colorado. And in the darkest of places and the most tragic of events, heroes emerged. They threw out all the rules. They did not wait for instructions. They followed the voice of their own soul—the one that always knows the next right thing. They were bigger than their fears. Some laid their bodies over others to protect them from bullets. Police officers broke rules and transported injured to hospitals, refusing to wait on ambulances. The human spirit lives and shines in the darkest of places, in the most tragic of events, and in the spaces where we are broken open.

Of this I am certain.

Life does not change you; it unfolds you.
—AUTHOR UNKNOWN

Unlearning and relearning.
Doors closing, doors opening—oops, not that door.
Holding on, letting go.
Asking hard questions, finding new answers.
Just breathe.

For a time, I thought that everything about my life had been wrong. But I learned that our lives are not right or wrong. They are constantly changing and unfolding and evolving. We are only wrong when we hold on to our "old skins" too long, preventing the process of change and transformation from occurring.

If I had not founded my failed business and spent my "trip to Italy" money transforming a tiny bungalow into an office that emerged as a safe haven to process and share the healing stories of lost jobs, lost lives, lost political aspirations, and lost dreams, I would have never been transformed by the stories of corporate executions—both those given and those received.

I would never have been part of the Transformation Tribe. They taught me to believe in things I cannot see and about the healing power of play and laughter, and they crystalized for me the incredible healing power of women and the tremendous leadership role they can play in building the new tomorrows.

I will forever be grateful for the lives that touched me so deeply as I hung *Bottom Side Up* and for those who nurtured me, shined their light into my darkness so that I could find my way back, and believed in me even when I didn't believe in myself.

And as if designed by someone else just for me, the last day of my AmeriCorp tour, I attended a chamber of commerce country club breakfast, complete with the crystal water glasses and the silver buffet line. Around the room were many of my former business friends and elected officials, but also there were many of my new friends, mental-health service providers, faith-based organizations that provided food for the hungry, and even a couple of homeless people. At overflow capacity, it was a sight to behold.

And the topic of conversation: homelessness in our community. With the many different interests in that room coming together to talk about solutions to community problems, I knew there had been another hole poked in the universe. That's just one more opportunity for light to shine in the darkest of places.

And that very same day, in the chamber of commerce packet on our table, was a notice of an economic summit, just like the one I had begged for four years ago. This one was hosted by none other than my friend, who was the new republican state legislator, and just two weeks earlier, he also brought in an eighteen-wheeler load of fresh fruits and vegetables as a food giveaway. And as a benediction to my AmeriCorp tour, a conservative friend of mine e-mailed me that he did something out of the ordinary for him. He had given his lunch to a homeless person.

Bottom Side Up

He wrote, "Linda, you're right. Life is fragile—for all of us."

Driving home from the chamber breakfast, I heard on the radio that Detroit had declared bankruptcy. I know some will say that it's a terrible thing. I think it is a painful but great opportunity to break open, fall apart, and come back as something else.

I say to all of us *Bottom-Side-Up* people, "Rise up; rise up from your ashes! Reclaim your passions. It is time.

> *You cannot connect the dots by looking forward;*
> *you can only connect them looking backward.*
> —STEVE JOBS

Four years ago, when I went into the back of the closet to paint, I was hiding. I did not intend to travel this path of self-discovery and radical transformation. After many moons of a self-imposed estrangement from the traditional establishment and the multitude of social props, I slowly realized that I had created space in my life to grow and to change and to hopefully one day return to my community to lead positive change.

Without the endless country club luncheons, award ceremonies, marketing messages and membership duties, I had begun to hear my own voice. I had found who I was when no one was looking.

It is possible that we can become more than spectators and consumers to blue states or red states.

We can actually become participators and producers. We can create health-care systems that nurture and support healthy communities. We can create education systems that wrap around the needs of the families and children of today. We can become beautiful, courageous, and wise actors in our own plays. We can re-story our own lives and our communities. We can reclaim our *Bottom Side Up*-ness. New life can spring up through the cracks in the places where we have been broken open—as my mama said, "If we can only muster the courage" to do so.

In the moments of my life that required unspeakable courage—burying my son, pushing the coffin of my mother, closing the doors of the chamber of commerce and saying good-bye to the place where I belonged, trying to forgive people that had betrayed me, taking our special-needs grandson to raise—those were some of the "life moments" that broke me open. It was up to me to have the courage to let my old life fall apart and have the courage to come back as something else.

> *She is not stifled by setbacks or paralyzed by fear.*
> *She uses life's challenges as exquisite opportunities*
> *to reexamine her vision, to reassess her gifts, and*
> *to summon back her light.*
> —"A FEARLESS WOMAN"

The light I reflect now is my own light. I do not know where the road will go. Will I be happy and healthy until I'm a hundred? I doubt it.

Will my face get lines and wrinkles? I'm pretty sure.

I'm also pretty sure I'm not getting botoxed.

Can I say with any certainty that I won't run away with the circus or do something really dumb, despite the wisdom life has bestowed upon me? No, not really.

Will I get betrayed again? I'm certain of it. It comes with the territory of living a life of passion, and now I accept that.

Will I get *Bottom Side Up* again? You can bet on it.

But most importantly, as Anne Lamontt writes in her book on *The Three Essential Prayers,*

"I have finally learned to say to the 'Something' that is far greater than me:

Help."

Thanks.

Wow.

EPILOGUE

By the time this book is released, I will have finished my tour with AmeriCorp and the National Homeless Coalition. I am forever grateful for the opportunity to have learned from some of the finest people in America on building organizational and community capacity and alleviating poverty and the effects of poverty in America.

My fierce entrepreneurial spirit helps me believe that America can rebuild itself. But we have a lot of work to do. The greatest lesson learned is that we must focus on developing and supporting stronger, more resilient, self-determined people. There is not enough money to continue the expansion of services for a culture that is uneducated, unemployed, sick, and addicted to drugs.

That means that we must educate our children, foster education systems of lifelong learning, create good jobs, and support and encourage health and wellness in ourselves, our families, and our communities.

Technology provides great opportunities to empower people through the creation of learning communities. It's an opportunity we must seize. These initiatives are transformational. My judge friend said, "If you push transformational projects, you should expect to get banged up, so pick your battles wisely." It's a lesson that I have learned well. And I'm hoping to get banged up again.

Having seen homelessness up close and knowing that it can happen to most of us in the blink of an eye, I have become radically grateful for every glass of cool clean water, every meal, my home, and my health. A thousand times a day, I whisper, "Thanks."

In the final half of my AmeriCorp tour, I was given the opportunity to study the trend in Florida and California of tent cities. It was then that I came to understand my unwavering confidence in the American dream. America is capable of building greater things than tent cities. Our compassion must not allow us to let people forget how to dream. Perhaps the American dream of our children will be a different dream from ours, but still, they must dream.

We must not let our "breaking open and falling apart" be the end of our story. We must find the courage to take the next step of "coming back as something else."

Do not go where the path my lead,
go instead where there is no path and leave a trail.
—RALPH WALDO EMERSON

Currently, I am serving as chairperson of one of the largest mental health and substance-abuse organizations in our county. We specialize in outpatient and inpatient treatment, but we also provide transitional and permanent housing opportunities for those who have re-storied their own lives. Most of the former "suits" are still my best friends, despite our awkward moments.

Our grandson is now in seventh grade. He is still not out of the woods. His mental-health issues make it very difficult for him to function in an education system that is fragile and chaotic and one that certainly was not created to serve as a wrap-around for special-needs children or their families. His journey will be upstream at best. But at least he has been in a loving and supportive environment, and that alone decreases his "at-risk factors."

My house is still crazily disorganized, and I still live with three messy males and a cat. I now consider myself a "reformed perfectionist." The cat still makes me itch, so we have developed some healthy boundaries. The guys still occasionally drink from the candle holders if they forget to wash their glass. I am still amused.

We are slowly learning to re-story our life. We are learning to set boundaries and to speak our truth as kindly as we can. Strangely, we have come to depend on each other—at least a little.

On my birthday, to mark my coming back as something else, I changed my political party affiliation to NPA (no party affiliation). I have spent time in both republican and democrat camps. I found good people and good ideas in both. When I was with Republicans, I longed for the inspiration and compassion of Mother Theresa and Dali Lama. When I was in the Democrat camp, I longed for the entrepreneurial business messages of Steve Jobs or Warren Buffet. I learned compassion and tolerance from the democrats and courage and the conservative way from the republicans. It seems to me like the best place is somewhere in the middle—where the two meet with compassion and courage.

Perhaps I will venture out again into the business world—perhaps not.

But if I do, I'll have a new dimension. I don't give a hoot about business titles or political affiliations or brands of religion. I want to know if you can still love your family and your friends even when things get *Bottom Side Up*.

I don't care how much is in your bank account; I want to know what's in your heart. I want to know the part of you that's left when all the trappings are gone. And mostly, I want to know if you have the courage to re-story your life when the one you have doesn't work anymore.

Don't tell me how you make your living; tell me how you make your life.

Bottom Side Up

And for the politicians, don't tell me how you talk your talk, show me how you walk your walk. Tell me how you re-storied your communities. Tell me how you gave your citizens something to believe in. Tell me how you created a new today that births a better tomorrow.

Writing this book forced me to condense a dozen years of my life into less than seventy-five thousand words. Owning your own story really takes you into the depths of the soul, discovering the things that really matter. I discovered the one theme in my life that remains constant. I am able to love fiercely in life's doorways of both coming and going.

That's no small thing.

And what about you?
When will you begin your long journey into yourself?
—Rumi

THE BEGINNING
Everything Is up for Grabs

BOTTOM SIDE UP WISDOM NUGGETS

Own your story.

Claim your experience by processing it—either on paper or by sharing it with someone you trust. It is important to your healing process to be able to tell your story in a safe place, without filtering it into something that you think is acceptable. (Do not tell your story on social media or with anyone you do not trust.) There are a lot of feelings in *Bottom Side Up*. They're all okay. Just own them and let them go. Remember what I told you: if you find yourself in hell, don't pitch a tent.

Find "Something" bigger than you.

Engage in whatever spiritual practice is right for you. Prayer, yoga, artwork, gardening, reading, etc. Mama taught me that life is too hard without help.

Take care of you. You're all you've got.

Be kind to your body. Eat healthy foods and get as much sleep and exercise as you can. See a mental health counselor or a doctor if your depression lingers.

Hold on to your old friends and make some new ones.

Seek out others who have been through similar situations. As you learned from the lessons from the bungalow, telling your story can be good medicine. Socialize as much as you can. Don't stay in the back of the closet painting for too long.

Be kind to others.

Channel your energy into something positive. Become active in your community. Volunteer at a pantry or food bank. The world needs you.

Don't forget to say thanks.

Cultivate gratitude; it is a miracle drug.
And above all, know that you are okay—*Bottom Side Up* and all.

NOTES FROM BOTTOM SIDE UP

NOTES FROM BOTTOM SIDE UP